A Practical Guide to Chronic Pain Claims

Pankaj Madan,
MA (Cantab), Barrister At Law,
Exchange Chambers, Leeds,
Manchester, Liverpool
& 12 King's Bench Walk, Temple, London

Law Brief Publishing

© Pankaj Madan

All rights reserved. No part of this publication may be reproduced, stored in a retrieval system, or transmitted, in any form or by any means, electronic, mechanical, photocopying, recording or otherwise, without the prior permission of the publisher.

Excerpts from judgments and statutes are Crown copyright. Any Crown Copyright material is reproduced with the permission of the Controller of OPSI and the Queen's Printer for Scotland. Some quotations may be licensed under the terms of the Open Government Licence (http://www.nationalarchives.gov.uk/doc/open-government-licence/version/3).

Cover image © iStockphoto.com/OGphoto

The information in this book was believed to be correct at the time of writing. All content is for information purposes only and is not intended as legal advice. No liability is accepted by either the publisher or author for any errors or omissions (whether negligent or not) that it may contain. Professional advice should always be obtained before applying any information to particular circumstances.

Published 2017 by
Law Brief Publishing
30 The Parks
Minehead
Somerset
TA24 8BT

www.lawbriefpublishing.com

Paperback: 978-1-911035-20-6

Thank you for buying this book. We are sure that you will find it informative and that the material will be a useful guide in the future. However, please note that the material must not be construed as advice on the interpretation and application of the law or procedure or medicine to particular circumstances, matters or cases and any such comments made by the author will not constitute and must not be relied upon as advice.

The material for this publication has been compiled solely for the purposes of the book and the benefit of the readers and as such does not necessarily stand on its own. The materials are not intended to be relied upon for giving specific advice.

To the extent permitted by law, neither the author, Pankaj Madan, Law Brief Publishing nor any other person will be liable by reason of breach of contract, negligence or otherwise for any loss or consequential loss occasioned to any person acting, omitting to act or refraining from acting in reliance upon the book material or presentation of the material. If and to the extent a Court disagrees, then any such loss or damage is limited to the price of the book, arising from or connected with any error or omission in the course material or presentation of the material. Consequential loss means any loss of anticipated profits, damage to reputation or goodwill. Loss of expected future business, damages costs or expenses payable to any third party or any other indirect losses. No part of the book may be reproduced without the prior permission of the author.

Should you require any further information about the author please visit: https://www.12kbw.co.uk/barristers/pankaj-madan/

For information on his published book in relation to Subtle Brain Injury Claims please visit:
http://www.lawbriefpublishing.com/SubtleBrainInjuryClaims/

Thank you and happy reading.

PREFACE

Over the past ten years there has been a substantial increase in the presentation of claims for personal injury arising out of seemingly minor accidents where long term pain and disability and substantial compensation are features. The claims often attract very substantial claims for damages approaching catastrophic values. This book attempts to understand from a Lawyer's perspective the medicine and the procedure and the Law needed to bring and defend such claims justly and at proportionate cost.

I must make it clear that I act for both Claimants and Defendants in largely equal measure and have no axe to grind. Although I am from a family of doctors, I am not a doctor. I make attempts as lawyers dealing with this should do, to understand the medicine behind the subject. It is a controversial subject where the doctors cannot agree upon the perpetuating factors behind chronic pain or even what may pre-dispose certain people to suffering from these conditions.

Litigation is a further complicating factor. Some claims arise from seemingly trivial or moderate accidents where a full recovery with modest damages would be expected. I apologise in advance therefore if I try to simplify the medicine. Undoubtedly, some doctors will disagree with my analysis. The aim is to enlighten this difficult area of personal injury law.

Pankaj Madan
April 2017

Contents

Chapter One	What is Pain?	1
Chapter Two	The Causes of Chronic Pain Disorder	5
Chapter Three	Recognising the Signs of Chronic Pain Disorder	11
Chapter Four	The Psychiatric Component	15
Chapter Five	Complex Regional Pain Syndrome	27
Chapter Six	Chronic Widespread Pain (CWP)	37
Chapter Seven	Causation	51
Chapter Eight	Bringing Chronic Pain Claims	67
Chapter Nine	Defending Chronic Pain Cases	79
Chapter Ten	Conclusions	97

CHAPTER ONE
WHAT IS PAIN?

The International Association for the Study of Pain (IASP) defines pain as:-

"an unpleasant sensory and emotional experience associated with actual or potential tissue damage, or described in terms of such damage".

There is no unanimity on the definition of "pain" but the consensus of medical opinion uses this IASP definition. Until 1979 there was no published definition. The key to understanding the definition is to note that firstly, whilst most patients with pain had tissue damage, the definition embodied the patients who had no identifiable tissue damage but nevertheless experienced pain.

Pain is an experience and therefore it is to a degree, subjective. Under the accepted medical IASP definition of pain, there is no pain which is imagined rather than real because pain is an experience.

It is important to remember that most pain is not chronic at all but transient. Even pain which is not transient usually resolves. Pain serves as a biological reminder of the dangers of the world in which we live and serves a useful function to keep us safe from danger or to alert us to dysfunction or disease within the body.

As pain is an experience it is not surprising that the attempts to classify and define pain have been made by both the World Health Organisation and the American Psychiatric Association. The World Health Organisation produce the International Classification of Disorders currently in its 10th edition. This is the so called "ICD10".

The American Psychiatric Association produce the Diagnostic and Statistical Manual of Mental Disorders, now in its fifth Edition commonly referred to as "DSM V"

The ICD10 Classification is the one most commonly used in the UK. It provides a classification of Pain Disorder and Persistent Somatoform Pain Disorder. The pain is a persistent, severe and distressing pain that cannot be fully explained by a physiological process or physical disorder. Traditional thinking is that the pain is presumed to be of a psychological origin.

Under the former DSM IV criteria, the word "somatoform" was dropped. The key point was that the pain could not be intentionally produced or feigned. There were two principal disorders:

"pain disorder associated with psychological factors,"

And

"pain disorder associated with both psychological factors and a general medical condition."

In this condition a physical condition may be present but not sufficient to account for the degree of pain experienced. Both psychological factors and a general medical condition are judged to have important roles in the onset, severity, exacerbation, or maintenance of the pain.

The latest DSM V Criteria has caused a degree of controversy in the psychiatric world. This now has a category called "Somatic Symptom Disorder" thereby removing four criteria of "somatisation Disorder", Hypochondriasis, Pain Disorder and "Undifferentiated Somatoform Disorder".

Patients must complain of at least one somatic symptom that is distressing or disruptive of their daily lives.

The Claimant must have at least one of the following:-

- emotional/cognitive behavioural disturbances:

- high levels of health anxiety,

- disproportionate and persistent concerns about the medical seriousness of the 'symptoms,' and

- an excessive amount of time and energy devoted to the symptoms and health concerns.

The duration of symptoms and later concerns must have lasted for at least six months."

Triggers for Chronic Pain

There are three principle triggers for "Chronic Pain". Firstly, it may be caused by a major or by a minor injury.

Secondly it can be a symptom of a painful or psychiatric medical condition not caused by a physical injury.

Thirdly, it may arise out of surgery or other deliberate medical intervention.

Unfortunately, the term "chronic pain" is not used consistently. It can refer to pain that has been present for a defined period of say 6 months or more or it can be a shortened term meaning "Chronic Pain Disorder". There are two terms in use that we need to define, "Chronic Pain Disorder" and "Chronic Pain Syndrome". They are not entirely the same.

> "*Chronic Pain Disorder*" is the presentation of combined physical and psychological changes which occur due to the presence of chronic pain.

> "*Chronic Pain Syndrome*" refers to persistent pain that usually has no identifiable source and is associated with abnormal illness behaviours, including expressions of pain, that are grossly disproportionate to any underlying cause.

It is hardly surprising that given such definitions and the adversarial system in which Claimants must prove their injury, and an age which brings considerable challenges in respect of the veracity of claims, that scepticism exists about the existence of Chronic Pain Disorder and Chronic Pain Syndrome.

As we will see there is a basis to chronic pain problems. It is not a fictitious condition. It very much occurs outside litigation and in the absence of discernible secondary gain factors but litigation also probably causes its own problems. The incidence of malingering or exaggeration in chronic pain cases within litigation approaches between 20 and 50% according to one study by Greve et Al conducted in 2009 but that is far short of all claims.

CHAPTER TWO
THE CAUSES OF CHRONIC PAIN DISORDER

Evidence based research suggests that when acute pain does not resolve within a few months, continued activation of nerves that transmit pain called "nociceptors" may result in changes in the spinal cord and brain that can lead to Chronic Pain Disorder or Chronic Pain Syndrome, or a heightened perception of pain. Some doctors have described it to me as the "volume switch" on the "amplifier" being turned up.

This mechanism may help explain why there is often some delay of several months in the presentation of the condition or even why soft tissue injuries appear to improve before becoming worse and gradually deteriorating. Far, therefore from being a sign of malingering, the delayed presentation of Chronic Pain may well be a sign of a genuine Claimant.

Pain signals from the nociceptors are processed in no fewer than seven centres of the brain. Pain is valuable and a primordial warning system of danger. As Porreca and Navratilova describe in their article entitled *"Reward, Motivation and Emotion of Pain and its relief" PAIN, Vol.158 April 2017,* the emotion of pain is a call to action like hunger, thirst or a desire to sleep. These pain signals are encoded in different sensory pathways and areas of the brain including the thalamus, insula and cingulate cortex. These cortical regions have connections with the valuation/decision "mesolimbic circuit" a part of the brain which integrates the information from multiple competing emotions and selects the behavioural action that offers the greatest benefit to the organism.

For all their research into this area they ultimately conclude that the knowledge of circuits in the brain that underlie pain remain understood only in a very basic way. Neuroimaging studies are beginning however to provide evidence of anatomical and neurological changes in these circuits in the setting of chronic pain where there has been long term stimulus by nociceptors. Put simply, if the pain signals being generated by the nociceptors become too much or last too long in certain individuals they can actually can damage the "amplifier" where the pain signals are being processed. The link between the "reward" circuits of the brain may have some profound implications for the world of personal injury. It may have to lead to the question whether the ability to be compensated and the compensation process could in some individuals, at least some of the time, be making the pain experience genuinely worse.

Certainly, the evidence for chronic pain because of changes in brain circuitry is growing. Modern brain neuroimaging techniques have revealed that patients with chronic back pain, neuropathic pain (that is pain arising from the dysfunction or damage to nerves themselves), fibromyalgia, irritable bowel syndrome, headache and complex regional pain syndrome have molecular, functional and anatomical or structural changes in the brain. In particular, there are abnormalities in grey matter density and in the connectivity of the white matter and differences in the transmission of certain neuro-transmitters. Some functional Magnetic Resonance Imaging studies have demonstrated that as pain becomes chronic there is a shift towards perception of the pain from the sensory regions to the regions of the brain associated with emotion.

Clients with Chronic Pain Disorder may ultimately have no *objective* signs upon physical examination. Their perception of pain and of incapacity depend on many variables, including character traits, personality, ethnic and cultural background, the presence of support systems, motivation and prior job satisfaction. Some people seem pre-disposed to suffer from greater and longer lasting pain. In law, that is known as "vulnerability". This is not a complete defence because as every lawyer and medico-legal expert knows, the tortfeasor "must take their victim as they find them". It may be a partial defence however and reduce damages.

Chronic Pain Disorder must be distinguished from a related condition called "***Complex Regional Pain Syndrome*** *(CRPS)* previously also called "Reflex Sympathetic Dystrophy", "Algodystrophy" or "Causalgia". This condition also involves chronic pain but is defined and diagnosed using a strict established set of criteria which will be dealt with later. Whilst Chronic Pain Disorder and CRPS may arise from the same vulnerability in the brain circuits they are different manifestations of a condition.

This is an interesting time for the understanding of Chronic Pain because the latest neuro-imaging techniques are allowing study of the pain mechanisms and pathways in the brain. The changes in the Central Nervous System due to prolonged pain may help to explain the disproportionate and non-dermatomal presentation of chronic pain.

The changes in the Central Nervous System and/or the direct trauma to the Nerve endings themselves in a soft tissue injury can lead to the development of another type of pain apart from the nociceptive pain above. This is "Neuropathic Pain"

According to Treede et al in 2012 "Neuropathic pain" is pain arising as a direct consequence of a lesion or disease affecting the somatosensory system. The circumstances in which a person develops chronic neuropathic pain are not well understood. There appears to be a poor correlation between the localisation or size of the lesion in the spinothalamic tract and degree of neuropathic pain.

The development of and presence of pain can now be verified due to the advent of high quality functional MRI studies albeit this is still not in widespread clinical use.

Neuropathic pain seems to occur with a variable delay after a lesion and does not generally occur in the acute phase of the lesion. Paradoxically it is, as the nerve or lesion begins to recover that the pain can become neuropathic leading some medical researchers to suggest that there is a dysfunctional re-organisation of the pain pathways in the brain and the spinal cord.

Peyron in his article in the Journal "Pain" entitled "*Functional Brain Imaging: what has it brought to our understanding of neuropathic pain?*" records his discovery that the "thalamus", an area of the brain associated with the perception of pain, had functional and structural abnormalities in people who were experiencing neuropathic pain conditions. There have also been reports of a focal brain lesion in brain injury cases leading to central pain disappearance. He concludes that further studies are needed.

There is also growing evidence that adverse events in childhood have a real correlation with chronic pain in later life. For example Jones, Power and MacFarlane in an article entitled *"Adverse Events in Childhood and Chronic Widespread Pain in Adult Life"* PAIN 143 (2009) 92-96 reported on several studies that showed that early life adversity is associated with Chronic Widespread Pain (CWP) in later life. Many of those studies were flawed however and the authors therefore undertook their own study. They assessed patients at 7 years by parental report and hospital records. They looked at poor social and psychological environment, periods in local authority care, death of a parent, parental divorce, alcoholism and financial hardship. Chronic Widespread pain was then assessed in that cohort of patients at 45 years of age using self-completion questionnaires. The study sample consisted of 7571 individuals. There was no association between childhood surgery and CWP in adulthood.

However, children who had been hospitalised following a road traffic accident experienced a significant increase in the risk of future CWP. Children who had been in institutional care also had an increase in risk as did those who suffered the death of a mother or familial financial hardship. These findings were not explained by adult psychological distress or social class.

There is now robust evidence that early life stress ("ELS") or childhood adversity is associated with increased vulnerability to a wide range of mental health and medical conditions. Sexual abuse, childhood abuse and neglect are associated with the onset of later adverse physiological responses to pain and stress. In other words, early life stress probably leads to long term alteration in responses to stress responsivity. There are some specific periods when the developing brain is particularly sensitive. There is also a dose response. In other words, the more the childhood adversity the greater the risk of adult chronic pain.

The type of ELS also matters. Different stresses affect different regions of the brain and the behavioural outcome. Research has shown that abuse prior to puberty has more selective effects upon the hippocampus whilst the pre-frontal cortex is significantly altered following abuse after puberty.

Some practitioners may have noticed a significant association between childhood abuse in the General Medical notes of a claimant who is suffering from chronic pain and wondered whether this was just a chance finding, or whether it was an indication of psychiatric vulnerability. The latest evidence shows that it is probably not a chance finding and that the best explanation may lie in the altered development of structures of the brain associated with pain.

In conclusion, Chronic Pain Disorder is a complex condition. Vulnerability to suffering Chronic or Widespread pain may have its roots in the alteration of the developing brain in childhood. There is a significant association between traumatic events in childhood such as sexual abuse, neglect, parental divorce, alcoholism and financial hardship and heightened pain response in adulthood. The latest research using functional MRI which can highlight activity in different centres of the brain is demonstrating altered structure and function in those individuals who suffer from Chronic Pain Disorder.

Because of all of this knowledge, a biopsychosocial approach to the assessment and management of pain has been recommended. Many psychosocial factors influence the development of chronic pain and how it progresses.

CHAPTER THREE
RECOGNISING THE SIGNS
OF CHRONIC PAIN DISORDER

Chronic Pain Disorder may or may not have an element of neuropathic pain. Alternatively, the pain may be all nociceptive.

Let us look at neuropathic pain in a little more detail. We have already defined neuropathic pain as referring to pain arising as a direct consequence of a lesion or disease affecting the somatosensory system. It is pain generated as result of damage or dysfunction of the nerves themselves either the peripheral or central nervous system, the system itself which signals pain. It is very difficult to treat.

Neuropathic pain has some not invariable distinguishing features which set it apart from nociceptive pain. These may be:-

- Prickling, tingling, pins and needles (dysesthesia)

- Electric shocks or shooting pains

- Hotness or burning sensations

- Ice cold sensations

- Numbness

- Pain evoked by light touching (a form of Allodynia (pain produced by a stimulus that does not normally evoke pain, such as a light touch with a feather.))

Unfortunately tests and advanced neuroimaging are still not universally accepted or standardised and there is no single or standard test for neuropathic pain. The most convenient approach is still to combine physical examination and the patient's own report. The reliance upon self-report makes for an interesting but often difficult journey during the course of litigation, for all concerned.

The point is that neuropathic pain may be triggered even by a seemingly minor insult to an area of previous injury that had healed without problem. Claimants with neuropathic pain as we have seen will usually report poorer physical and mental health even compared with clients with ordinary nociceptive only pain and the previous chapter provides the research which may help us understand why this is the case.

Neuropathic pain cannot usually be treated effectively using standard pain relieving medication like paracetamol or ibuprofen. A good initial indicator therefore that you may be dealing with a case of neuropathic pain and perhaps therefore a case of chronic pain Disorder or Chronic Pain Syndrome can therefore be gleaned from a thorough examination of a Claimant's medical and physiotherapy notes about the distribution, pattern and *sensations* of their pain. As far as medication as an indicator goes the following medications are all used to treat neuropathic pain:-

- Amitriptyline,
- Serotonin and norepinephrine reuptake inhibitors (e.g. Duloxetine and Venlafaxine)
- Anticonvulsants
    - Carbamazepine,
    - Pregabalin,
    - Gabapentin,
    - Valproate,
- Opioids,
- Capsaicin Cream,
- Lignocaine Plasters

CHAPTER THREE – RECOGNISING THE SIGNS OF CHRONIC PAIN DISORDER • 13

It is worth remembering however that early diagnosis of this condition is rare. The Claimant may not have received any specialist treatment as yet. Indeed, often months or years pass before referral to the Chronic Pain Expert. Sometimes such referral never occurs.

In summary, the best indications at an early stage of Chronic Pain Disorder are likely to be that:

- The pain that has improved and then worsened in a matter of months after the initial accident,

- The pain is out of proportion to the initial stimulus or accident in question;

- The usual form of pain relieving medications have not worked and the set of symptoms of burning sensations or allodynia (sensitivity to touch) have manifested themselves.

- There is a history of Early Life Stress.

It is worth noting that victims of chronic pain disorder (but not CPRS) after an accident have often previously:-

- Consulted their GP more than average in the past;

- Often had "somatic" complaints in the past where no known physical cause was found for past pain.

Chronic Pain Disorder occurs in both sexes but is slightly more prevalent statistically in females.

CHAPTER FOUR
THE PSYCHIATRIC COMPONENT

We have already looked at the definition of pain in Chapter 1. The reader will recall that it is is an unpleasant *emotional* experience. Pain is an emotion and pain signals are interpreted in the brain. Medicine is now learning more about organic dysfunctional pain pathways in the brain.

It is difficult therefore to disentangle the psychogenic elements of Chronic Pain Disorder from the experience of pain. There is or usually has been an organic generator, pain signals, being generated in the tissues say for example in the neck or the back or a limb.

So far, we have examined those signals being heightened and sometimes perpetuated after the organic stimulating injury should have healed.

Somatic Symptom Disorder

There are conditions however where the pain is not thought to be organically generated and never was organically generated.

Somatic symptom disorder (SSD) and other disorders with prominent somatic symptoms constitute a new category in DSM-5 called somatic symptom and related disorders. The conditions specified in the chapter are as follows:-

- Somatic Symptom Disorder

- Illness Anxiety Disorder

- Conversion Disorder (Functional Neurological Symptom Disorder)

- Psychological Factors Affecting Other Medical Conditions

- Factitious Disorder

- Other Specified Somatic Symptom and Related Disorder

- Unspecified Somatic Symptom and Related Disorder

All the disorders in this chapter share a common feature: the prominence of somatic symptoms associated with significant distress and impairment. The DSM IV diagnoses of hypochondriasis, pain disorder and undifferentiated somatoform disorder have been removed to be subsumed under the heading of SSD.

If the Claimant is pre-occupied with their health to an excessive degree and experiencing distress, a diagnosis of a somatic symptom disorder rather than a chronic pain disorder may apply. There may a diagnosis of DSM V SSD based on:-

- the Claimant's psychological reaction to the physical symptoms together with,

- disproportionate and persistent thoughts about the seriousness of symptoms,

- persistent high levels of anxiety about health and

- excessive time and energy devoted to these symptoms or health concerns.

Strangely, there is no requirement that there is an unexplained medical condition. This seems perverse and some psychiatrists are critical of the new criteria.

Somatic symptoms may have very strange effects. I have had a claimant who after a 5-10 mph accident in a car park took to a wheelchair and never used their legs to bear weight again. The Defendant eventually accepted that the Claimant was genuine and the claim settled for a significant sum.

I have also had a case where the client walked like a crab with their arms above their heads. I watched as the client walked in sideways into the conference room, arms above their head. The Claimant was convinced of a brain injury. Medical science had no organic explanation for these conditions and their condition was explicable only as a somatic symptom disorder but compensable nevertheless.

With Somatic Symptom Disorder, secondary gain is often a perpetuating factor although often sub-conscious. If it is not sub-conscious and it is deliberate, then this is the fine line between Somatic Symptom Disorder and malingering. There are shades of grey in this area.

There is a very interesting and helpful article by Dr Leigh Neal, Consultant Psychiatrist and Dr Jon Valentine, *"Medically unexplained Pain in Personal Injury Litigation, Personal Injury Law Journal 117 2-8.*

They record that the characteristics of a somatic disorder can probably be summarised as follows: -

- There may be features of pre-existing abnormal personality;

- There are often multiple, fluctuating and medically organically unexplained symptoms for which the Claimant has consulted for medical opinion;

- Consequentially the Claimant's medical notes are usually voluminous;

- They have however rarely been seen or diagnosed by a psychiatrist before the legal claim;

Under the DSM V criteria for Somatic Symptom Disorder, it was recognised that there is a limitation to excluding the organic explanation. Therefore, the diagnosis is based on the claimant's psychological reaction to the physical symptoms. There are disproportionate and persistent thoughts about the seriousness of the symptoms and persistent high levels of anxiety about health or symptoms and excessive time and energy devoted to those symptoms or health concerns.

The new ICD-11 soon to replace ICD 10 in 2018 is likely to have a category of "Body Distress Disorder" which would encompass such symptoms.

Chronic Pain Disorder can therefore be a continuum with a purely psychological cause at one extreme and a purely organic cause (often with at least an element of neuropathic pain) at the other extreme. Even when the pain is organically generated however there are usually psychiatric factors also at play because the experience of pain on a continual basis may cause changes in mood, bio-chemical changes at a molecular level in the brain and dysfunction and structural changes in the pain pathways and the different pain processing centres in the brain.

Diagram: Showing a Continuum

Organic   Psychological

◄───►

CHRONIC PAIN DISORDER/SYNDROME

I have tended to notice that more psychiatrists tend to use the term "Chronic Pain Disorder" and Pain Management or Chronic Pain Specialists (usually anaesthetists) or Rheumatologists tend to use the term "Chronic Pain Syndrome". Sometimes, the terms are used interchangeably but they are not quite the same as we have seen.

Why might a Claimant develop psychological maintenance or exacerbation of pain? The recent research which I have described in previous chapters may lead the reader to conclude that it may be caused by the changes in the pain pathways. Manek and McGregor found that 90% of patients with chronic low back pain do not have any reliable indicators of physiological or anatomical deficit. Of course, such organic stressors may be at a level which is not capable of being resolved on MRI scanning. But what else may cause the alteration in mood and the changes which may lead to the perpetuation of pain?

Secondary gain may also be a factor. Because pain is a primordial response, it is not inconceivable that the sub-conscious knowledge that continuing pain may be rewarded helps to perpetuate the pain experience. Secondary gain may take many forms:

- the continuation of attention and care from a third party such as a spouse or friend;

- the knowledge the Claimant won't have to return to a job or former life they didn't particularly like,

- any knowledge that the longer the pain continues then potentially the greater the compensation,

- compensation from a salary insurance scheme or state benefits.

The legal profession and insurance industry both may be unwittingly contributing to the pain experience. One major insurer's representative posed an interesting question at a recent meeting – "Why do Claimant Solicitors measure success by the size of the settlement or award?"

It's a good question. More emphasis on rehabilitation, restoration of function and amelioration of pain and an early settlement probably ought to be measures of success but they are not so succinctly enunciated or appreciated in marketing material. The Government through the doctrine of "proportionality" have linked success and recovery of fees to the size of the claim. These claims are complex whether they are big claims or more limited in value.

The undoubted stress of the adversarial experience and the suspicion which claimants are soon placed under probably does not help either. As the condition fails to get better quickly or within the expected time frame claimants also must bear the following:-

- Anxiety over loss of earnings and consequent inability to pay bills or a mortgage;

- Lack of sleep caused by pain. Sleep deprivation over many weeks, months or even years may be contributing to those biochemical and structural changes in the Central Nervous System;

- Fear that activity is damaging may lead to restriction of activity and subsequent physical de-conditioning;

- Misattribution and catastrophic pain behaviour;

- Failure to accept the condition;

- Social isolation and loss of status;

- An adversarial legal system.

Does Money Matter?

The fact of compensation may form part of the secondary gain processes at least in some people some of the time. The primordial pathway perpetuates responses to experiences which may be rewarding. Pain may be one of those experiences.

Rohling and Binder in a study reported in an article entitled *"Money matters. A meta-analytic review of the Association between financial Compensation and the Experience and the treatment of Chronic Pain"* as far back as 1995 found that rates of people seeking compensation for low back pain had increased by 2,680% between 1960 and 1980. Logically, compensation should have no effect upon the patient's pain experience. However, pain is a subset of behaviour and subject to the same principles of positive and negative reinforcement. But that doesn't mean it's conscious or malingering or exaggeration. Not necessarily anyway.

However, the presence of depression, financial worries, emotional and financial instability caused by the accident can heighten the perception of pain.

The researchers found therefore that the compensation process results in an increase in pain perception and a reduction in the ability to benefit from medical treatment.

What does claiming compensation do to outcome?

One might expect that injury compensation would leave injured parties better off than they would otherwise have been but some think that claiming compensation does more harm than good. There is some evidence for and against this so it is important to take a broad look at the literature. Fortunately, Spearing et al did this in 2010.

In an article entitled *"Does injury compensation lead to worse health after whiplash? A systematic review"* Pain, 153 (2012) 1274-1282, the researchers Spearing, Connelling, Gargett and Sterling reviewed the evidence on this compensation hypothesis in relation to compensable whiplash injuries. They reviewed all the major e-databases of medical research articles from their inception to April 2010 comparing health outcomes of adults exposed to compensation related factors compared to those who were not exposed. They examined the effect of lawyer involvement, litigation, claim submission or previous claims on pain and other health outcomes. Among the 16 results reported were 9 significant *negative* associations between compensation related factors and health outcomes. Their conclusion was that there was *no clear evidence* to support the idea that compensation and its related processes lead to worse health. They also warned against the use of such evidence to avoid ineffectual and potentially harmful policy and judicial decisions.

Sterling et al in an article published in 2010 in Pain *"Compensation claim lodgement and health outcome developmental trajectories following whiplash injury: A prospective study"* evaluated 155 patients with whiplash and PTSD type symptoms. The patients were evaluated at 1 month, 3, 6, and 12 months post-injury. Outcomes at each point were assessed under the Neck Disability Index scoring system and the Post-traumatic stress diagnostic scale. The analyses were then repeated in the presence of third party compensation claim lodgement.

Three distinct NDI trajectories were determined. Mild, moderate and chronic-severe.

The NDI (Neck Disability Index) Scores of both the mild and moderate trajectories increased by 8-10% in the presence of litigation.

The researchers found that making a claim for compensation within 12 months **was** associated with an increase in symptoms.

Those that would have recovered well continued to report ongoing mild pain and disability during those 12 months.

Those who were going to be left with mild to moderate pain were left with pain estimated to be moderate during those 12 months.

This change did NOT extend however to those exhibiting Chronic-Severe symptoms.

In this category, there was no significant association or alteration of pain levels or duration with claim lodgement as opposed to the sample with no claims lodgement.

Spearing et al concluded in an article in the Journal of Clinical Epidemiology in 2012 65 (2012) 1219-1226 that baseline scores of neck pain were worse in claimants than non-claimants. In other words, the severity of the injury and pain was an important factor in causing somebody to make a claim for compensation. This is called "**Reverse Causality**". Therefore, research suggesting that claimants fared worse than non-claimants was fundamentally flawed. It is important to consider and eliminate the so called "reverse causality" effect. It is probably those who suffer with more severe pain and consequences who are more likely to make a claim. They found then when reverse causality is ignored claimants appeared to do worse than non-claimants. However, when reverse causality was considered, claiming compensation appeared to have a beneficial effect on recovery. They felt that access to good quality treatment may have been responsible for that beneficial effect.

The ending of the case

It is often said that ending the case will assist the Claimant to recovery. It has a certain attractiveness for the insurer particularly and sometimes the Claimant's team as well. It seems to make sense particularly if the stress of litigation may be a perpetuating factor. Your view on this may depend on which side of the fence you inhabit. But what does the literature say?

Spearing and Connelly in their study reported in the article "*Is Compensation bad for health. – A systematic meta-review*" studied 11 major papers. They concluded that:-

- 9 of the 11 papers were low quality studies which suffered from methodological weaknesses.

- Amongst 3 papers, 2 reviews concluded that compensation is a mediating factor in whiplash recovery; Claim duration was a proxy for recovery.

- The review by Scholten-Peeters in 2003 reported in the Journal "Pain" however specifically limited the focus to measures of symptoms and disability and was a high-quality study. It found strong evidence *of no association* between the legal process and recovery from whiplash injury.

- The study was funded by the Motor Accident Insurance Commission, Queensland, Australia without restriction.

They concluded that moves to design and limit compensation schemes on the basis that they were bad for health were premature as evidence of an association was unclear.

The reader will perhaps have to form their own conclusions upon the likelihood of the cessation of litigation leading to an improvement in the claimant.

So, what works?

The best solution seems to be cognitive behavioural therapy. Yes, talking to the brain can help reverse the structural and functional changes which have occurred because of pre-accident stressors and the stress and organic injuries arising from the accident. Several studies had reported reduced cerebral grey matter volume or density in chronic pain conditions. There had been limited research on the plasticity of the human cortex in response to psychological interventions. Seminowicz et al took a mixed group of chronic pain patients and gave them an 11 week CBT treatment programme and compared them with a control group. They found increased grey matter in various areas of the brain. Decreased pain catastrophising was associated with increased grey matter in various areas associated with pain perception. They hypothesised that CBT was resulting in greater top-down control over pain and cognitive re-appraisal of pain. When we consider the most recent evidence using functional MRI it may not just be top-down pain control but perhaps it is directly operating on the centres of the brain responsible for the cause of the pain. In other words, some are beginning to look at chronic pain as a type of "subtle brain injury" or deficit. The brain is now being seen as something which is *neuroplastic*. The brain responds to experience and changes and stressors in environment and its structure and biochemical make up changes too. The changes which caused pain appear however to be reversible and CBT appears to be a valuable tool.

It is always difficult to summarise such a complex and controversial topic. My interpretation of the literature I have seen to date suggests to me as follows:-

- There is often a psychiatric component to the pain.

- Most Chronic Pain Disorder cases are a complex interrelationship between the organic stressor and psychiatric consequences.

- Many chronic pain victims were vulnerable to the development of chronic pain.

- Some chronic pain cases appear to be almost completely psychiatrically generated with minimal or no organic cause.

- At one extreme, the case may be entirely somatic and an appropriate diagnosis may be a somatic symptom disorder or other related condition under the DSM V criteria.

- The scientific evidence that litigation promotes or maintains the claim is poor once "reverse causality" is taken account of.

- There is poor evidence that there are worse health outcomes because of litigation.

- There is a poor evidence base for dramatic-improvement, post-litigation particularly in the absence of treatment.

- There is a growing evidence base for grey matter changes in the brain's pain processing centres in cases of chronic pain disorder.

- Cognitive Behaviour Therapy has some success in treating the causes of chronic pain as well as helping people deal with its effects.

CHAPTER FIVE
COMPLEX REGIONAL PAIN SYNDROME

This is sometimes mis-referred to as "chronic regional pain syndrome". This is a misnomer and a condition which simply does not exist. Few who truly specialise in this area would be likely to make this mistake.

Complex Regional Pain Syndrome is a specific pain condition. It is a disorder of the extremities and is very much at the organic end of the spectrum as it results in very visible changes. It often used to be called "Reflex Sympathetic Dystrophy" or "Causalgia". It is certainly not a new condition. It affects people most commonly between the ages of 30 to 60 but any age can be affected and it affects female patients more than males. Of those affected by limb trauma, about 5% may develop symptoms of CRPS. There may be a genetic component or vulnerability in the brain pain processing circuits. Most cases are associated with trauma or surgery but up to one third of cases have no provoking event.

It is characterised by swelling, autonomic and motor and trophic changes. The pathology of CRPS remains poorly understood but it is thought to have a higher central nervous system origin particularly in some of those structures in the brain that we have already discussed. It can only occur in a limb. You don't get CRPS of the back or neck or trunk.

Some research doctors think that the anterior cingulate cortex (ACC) and periaqueductal grey (PAG) a mid-brain structure may be involved. Stimulation of the PAG inhibits pain signals. Dysfunction in both areas can result in the PAG failing to inhibit pain signals. Instead of a negative quiescent response, the response becomes a positive feedback cycle encouraging the injured area to become more swollen, more painful and more inflamed due to over activity of the parasympathetic nervous system. There is a strong association between Post-Traumatic Stress Disorder and the condition.

The development of the condition

A likely scenario is as follows:

Stage 1

The original injury or trauma initiates a gate impulse along the nerves carried by sensory nerves to the central nervous system.

Stage 2

The pain impulse in turn triggers an impulse in the sympathetic nervous system which returns to the original site of the injury.

Stage 3

The sympathetic nervous impulse triggers the inflammatory response causing the vessels to spasm leading to swelling and increased pain. The resulting condition is often burning pain and red mottling of the skin.

Stage 4

The pain triggers another response establishing a vicious cycle of pain and swelling.

CRPS has a very specific definition and signs. It is sometimes seen because of a crushing injury or in phantom limb pain after amputation or after a fracture.

The essential characteristics of the condition are:

- pain,
- sensory abnormalities,
- swelling,
- stiffness,
- motor dysfunction,

- trophic changes,

- symptoms such as temperature differences,

- skin colour differences,

- such as purple or red colouring,

- sweating,

- abnormal sensitivity to heat or cold.

A set of the symptoms set out above may provide a clue to the lawyer that a claimant is suffering from CRPS and to obtain specific evidence from a pain expert.

The specific criteria are as follows:-

Firstly, there must be continuing pain which is disproportionate to any inciting event.

Secondly the Claimant must report at least one symptom in three of the four following categories:-

Sensory – Reports of hyperesthesia and/or allodynia

Vasomotor – Reports of temperature differences and/or skin colour changes and/or skin colour asymmetry

Sudomotor – Reports of sweating changes or asymmetry in sweating

Motor/trophic changes – Reports of decreased range of motion and/or motor dysfunction (weakness, tremors) and/or trophic changes meaning changes to the hair, nails and skin.

Finally, there must be no other diagnosis that better explains the condition.

The criteria for the formal diagnosis of CRPS are called the "Budapest Criteria".

There are at least two types of CRPS, I and II. The major differences are these:-

CRPS II always needs a precipitating event. CRPS I might occur spontaneously.

CRPS II always has single peripheral nerve involvement.

CRPS II does not have physiologic changes in the limb.

The Cardinal signs are different.

CRPS I is characterised by spontaneous pain, swelling and different skin temperatures.

CRPS II is characterised by burning pain, allodynia (perception of pain to stimuli which would not normally cause pain, e.g. stroking with a feather) and Hyperalgesia.

CRPS I is always progressive and always causes bony atrophy.

CRPS II may be progressive but will not cause bony atrophy.

Evidence based research shows that in general, CRPS patients display significantly greater acute pain sensitivity (lower heat pain threshold) compared to non-CRPS patients. They are also significantly more sensitive to non-noxious warmth and cold. There were also measurable temperature differences between the affected side and unaffected side.

Berlein found that Complex regional pain syndrome (CRPS) may develop after limb trauma and is characterised by pain, sensory-motor and autonomic symptoms. Most important for the understanding of the pathophysiology of CRPS are recent results of neurophysiological research. Major mechanisms for CRPS symptoms, which might be present subsequently or in parallel during CRPS, are trauma-related cytokine release, exaggerated neurogenic inflammation, sympathetically maintained pain and cortical reorganisation in response to chronic pain (neuroplasticity).

CRPS and outcome

- 10% of Patients cannot recall any specific trauma.

- The initiating traumatic event may be trivial.

- 7% can spread to other limbs (**Provisional Damages claims should probably be the norm if there is a true diagnosis of CRPS**).

- 15% do not get better after 2 years.

Onset and Causation

There is usually a delay between the traumatic event and the onset of CRPS. The onset ranges from immediately to 12 months from a traumatic event as illustrated in the following studies.

- Dunningham in 1976-79 found a mean duration of onset of 18 weeks.

- Ohabayashi et al found that the mean onset was 18 weeks with a range of 8-52 weeks.

- Roganovic found the mean onset to be 2.6 days after injury.

- Tountas and Nogouchi found it was 2.5 months after injury.

- Veldman discounted any causation where injury is over 1 year from onset of the condition.

- Spontaneous onset without any traumatic event or surgery occurs in 3-11% of cases, often in a younger group of people.

Outcome

It is important to remember that most cases of CRPS get better quickly. Only:-

15% have pain after 2 years,

90% are better at 2 years.

There is a significant minority that don't get better or claim not to have got better. These are the cases we are most likely to see in high value litigation. Sometimes CRPS is replaced with a potentially new 3rd type of CRPS called "NOS" meaning "not otherwise specified".

It is like a residual CRPS condition from which CRPS in its true sense can flare up from time to time. Furthermore, true CRPS is sometimes better but replaced with functional or psychological effects better referred to as a chronic pain disorder or syndrome or of course outright exaggeration and malingering.

Complex Regional Pain Syndrome may be thought to be often easier to manage from a lawyer's point of view due to its organicity but it is just as controversial.

The condition is medico-legally very complex and often very high value. There will often be claims for Provisional Damages with an initial monetary value of more than £1 million.

The symptoms should include definite physical signs that can be seen or measured or felt. It is often the temperature differential between the affected side and unaffected side which tends to provide the key element of the diagnosis. Thermography uses an infra-red heat seeking camera or video to measure the infra-red heat emitted from a part of the body. Significant temperature differences between two limbs is suggestive of CRPS.

Can symptoms be feigned?

The short answer is yes. It is possible (though it takes a considerable effort) to feign symptoms of CRPS. *Singh & Davis*[1] found that the effects of short-term dependency and immobility on skin temperature could be influenced by hanging the arm dependent and motionless while using the right hand for light office work. After 30 minutes the dependent left hands were cooler by on average 0.9 degrees C than the active right hands. The left hand also exhibited a deeper colour.

In a second study, seven volunteers submerged both their hands in water at 15 degrees C for 15 minutes. The left arm was then left dependent and motionless while the right hand was placed on the table and fingers were flexed and extended every 10 seconds. The left hands remained cooler than the right and were a median of 2.9 to 4.5 degrees' Celsius cooler after 60 minutes. These studies showed that at least some skin temperature differences often used to conclusively state that somebody must have CRPS, can be intentionally produced by short term immobility and dependency of the hand.

Treatment

The best course of treatment is early identification together with Cognitive Behavioural Therapy, medication and intensive physiop- therapy and hydrotherapy in combination. Normal pain relieving medication such as ibuprofen may be of some use in controlling mild pain. Normally. Gabapentin or Pre-Gabalin are prescribed. None of these drugs are licenced for the treatment of neuropathic pain or CRPS but in randomised controlled trials involving patients with neuropathic pain (Non-CRPS) have shown a modicum of success though hardly striking success. The average pain score for those on a dose of 2,400 mgs per day of Gabapentin decreased by 21% (1.5 points on the scale) compared to 14% reduction in the placebo-treated patients.

---

1 The effect of short-term dependency and immobility on skin temper- ature and colour in the hand 13th January 2006. H.P Singh and T.R.C. Davis

I have asked many a claimant whether the Gabapentin or Pre-Gabalin works. Many are just not sure. They take it because they've been told to take it and they've never stopped.

Most are desperate for something to help alleviate the pain and if it helps a little, they will continue to take the drug provided the side effects are not too severe. Some say it helps but they can't tolerate the side effects. Most reply that it doesn't take the pain away completely but that it just takes "the edge off" the pain.

Carbamezipine is also sometimes prescribed for such pain.

Gabapentin and Carbamezipine are licenced for epilepsy. They are designed to cross the Blood Brain Barrier and act on the brain, centrally.

There are other medications. In fact, the only striking point is that no one thing works in all people all of the time. Sometimes, nothing seems to work.

Treatment therefore seems to consist of trial and error, calcitonin, bisphosphonates, and Clonidine. Dr Rajesh Munglani, a well-known leading pain expert tells the story of treating one patient with Clonidine by infusion. He watched as the patient's swelling and symptoms disappeared over the course of several hours. In another patient it just has no effect.

Patients with cutaneous changes or a persistent motion loss in a limb may require a regional nerve block. Stellate ganglion blocks or intravenous regional (Bier) blocks are also sometimes used.

Where a limb is profoundly affected and degenerates, ulcerates and potentially becomes gangrenous sometimes the only treatment left, sadly, is amputation. It should be emphasised that this is a treatment of last resort to save life, not a cure for the CRPS. Indeed, patients often continue to report phantom limb pain long after the limb has been amputated.

Because of the risk of spreading and the risk of potential amputation after worsening of the conditions therefore practitioners should always question experts carefully about the risks involved. Risks are usually greater than 1% and therefore provisional damages awards are usually essential in cases of true continuing CRPS.

The secondary gain may not be obvious

In an article by Burke *"Factitious Disorders of the Upper Limb"*[2], it was estimated that deception rates in personal injury claims generally were around 30%. This was more than deception rates in Criminal Cases, assessed at 19%.

Tourniquet-induced swelling should be considered in the medico-legal context. The causes may also be more subtle, psychiatric but genuine.

Disuse or alteration of use of a limb over time due to psychiatric effects or belief of injury can result in the development of CRPS. In other words, CRPS may stem from a belief of CRPS or Chronic Pain or Injury. It can become a self-fulfilling prophecy.

The "psycho-flexed hand" is a type of self-contracture with claims of disuse.

The "Belle Indifference", often characterised by an inappropriate smirk or smiling upon examination may also be a potential sign of a factitious disorder. Factitious disorder is a diagnosis under the DSM V criteria. "Burke" wrote that the secondary gain may not always be obvious. He gives the example of a schoolboy who presented with a demarcated lesion tip to the index finger of his dominant hand. It turned out it was caused by him applying an elastic band to the finger in bed each night with the effect and intention that it would get him out of school. The boy was being bullied at school and the intended deception was with a view to avoiding this distress. Burke stated that financial reward and compensation are more obvious forms of gain provoking exaggeration and malingering.

---

[2] The Journal of Hand Surgery Vol. 33E Np.2 April 2008

CHAPTER SIX
CHRONIC WIDESPREAD PAIN (CWP)

This is yet another sub-set of Chronic Pain. CWP encompasses at least two well-known conditions, Fibromyalgia and Chronic Fatigue Syndrome (CFS) but the modern term encompassing all such conditions is "chronic widespread pain".

We frequently encounter cases involving the development of widespread chronic pain after an initial injury for example to the neck or the back. It occurs with consequent disability and distress.

Both conditions are multi-symptomatic syndromes with the following core features:-

- Chronic widespread pain,

- Chronic unexplained fatigue.

Fibromyalgia is about 4 times more common in women than in men. (2% versus 0.5%). There is a steady increase in those affected according to age. It was once thought that there was either some lesion or disease in muscle or nerve tissue or that there were hormonal changes which were responsible. In fact, there is now good evidence that CWP is again caused by abnormal sensory processing within the central nervous system due to magnification of peripheral sensory input.

FM sufferers also tend to report with a higher incidence than normal the following symptoms:-

- Low back pain

- Recurrent headaches

- Arthritis

- Muscle spasm

- Tingling
- Balance problems
- Irritable bowel syndrome
- Numbness
- Chronic fatigue
- Bloating
- Depression
- Anxiety
- Sinus problems
- Tooth disorders
- Restless legs
- Tinnitus
- Jaw pain
- Bladder problems
- Rashes

These problems may also be explained by central sensitivity problems in the brain.

FMS is also found in accompaniment to other painful disorders such as rheumatoid arthritis, migraine, low back pain, systematic lupus erythematosus and inflammatory bowel disease.

There is a strong association with post-traumatic stress disorder and again there is an association in the literature with childhood trauma and sexual abuse.

The American College of Rheumatology requires persistent symptoms of 3 months' duration and widespread pain accompanied by tenderness at 11 of 18 tender point locations.

- Occiput:

- Low cervical: at C5-C7

- Trapezius: bilateral, at the midpoint of the upper border

- Supraspinatus: bilateral, at the origins, above the scapular spine near the medial border

- Second rib: bilateral, at the second costochondral junctions

- Lateral epicondyle: bilateral, 2cm distal to the epicondyles

- Gluteal: bilateral, in the upper outer quadrants of the buttocks in the anterior fold of muscle

- Greater trochanter: bilateral, posterior to the trochanteric prominence

- Knee: bilateral, at the medial fat pad proximal to the joint line

More recent criteria have indicated a diagnosis based on common pain locations and common symptoms.

The development of widespread pain following whiplash injury is in fact well documented. The Buskila study in 1997 studied 102 patients with neck trauma. 90% had been subject to classic whiplash type injuries. A control group of 59 patients had been subjected to leg trauma. These were the findings:-

- Although no patient had a chronic pain syndrome prior to the trauma, FMS was diagnosed following injury in 21.6% of those with neck injury versus 1.7% of the control patients with lower extremity fractures.

- Almost all symptoms were more common and severe in the group with neck injury. FM was noted at a mean of 3.2 months (SD 1.1) after the trauma. Neck injury patients with FM had more tenderness, had more severe and prevalent FM-related symptoms, and reported lower quality of life and more impaired physical functioning than did those without FM.

- Despite the injury or the presence of FM, all patients were employed at the time of examination. Twenty percent of patients with neck injury and 24% of patients with leg fractures filed an insurance claim. Claims were not associated with the presence of FMS, increased FM symptoms, pain, or impaired functioning.

We can draw the following conclusions from the study:-

- FM was 13 times more frequent following neck injury than following lower extremity injury. All patients continued to be employed, and insurance claims were not increased in patients with FM.

The study is often cited by the Claimant's medico-legal expert but in fact the study has been criticised and to some extent discredited.

The *Allaf and Dunbar Study* in 2002[1] examined the role of physical trauma in the onset of fibromyalgia.

The results were quite startling. They found that 39% of FMS patients reported significant physical trauma in the 6 months before the onset of their disease compared with only 24% of controls. They concluded that there was a "significant association" between physical trauma in the preceding 6 months and the onset of FMS.

---

1 A Case-Control Study examining the role of physical trauma in the onset of fibromyalgia syndrome.

By Contrast the study by Wynne-Jones et al *"Predicting New Onset of Widespread Pain following a Motor Vehicle Collision"* reported in the *Journal Of Rheumatology 2006, Volume 33 No.5* found that few collision specific factors predicted the onset of widespread pain. In contrast, they found that:-

- Pre-collision health seeking behaviour was more important i.e. if the patient went to their doctor a lot before the accident they tended to do worse;

- If they "somatised" before the accident with organic complaints for which no cause was found from a physical perspective those people tended to do worse;

- If they were told or believed they were severely injured they tended to do worse; (will the police ever stop telling people they are "lucky to be alive"? Does this help?)

- Older people tended to do worse;

- In combination, these factors accounted for a 20-fold difference in the onset of chronic widespread pain.

Results from the Epifund Study showed that pre-accident psychosocial factors were much more important in predicting the development of Chronic Widespread Pain.

This seems to fit well with a more general study by Castensen et al, *"Sick Leave within 5 years of Whiplash Trauma predicts Recovery: A Prospective Cohort and Register-Based study"* showed that if the patient took a lot of sick leave and didn't particularly enjoy their job before the accident or event in question then they were more likely to not to return to work due to pain. Sick leave before the collision therefore predicted strongly more prolonged rates of recovery following whiplash.

Is this malingering or is it vulnerability?

That is the key question in most cases and a question which only the trial judge in a case can ultimately answer and even then, rarely to the satisfaction of both sides in the case.

Is it all in the mind however?

As we have seen in relation to other conditions, probably not. The study *by Banic and Petersen-Felix et al* reported in Pain in 2004 demonstrated evidence for spinal cord hyper-sensitivity in chronic pain and in fibromyalgia. This can cause increased pain when stimulated with low dose pain signals which would usually not generate a pain response. In other words, is this the evidence again of the "volume switch" being turned up.

Overall, a number of studies have provided an association between febrile illness and trauma and the onset of FMS. Functional MRI studies are now demonstrating that there is evidence of dysfunction in the pain processing pathways in the brain. This provides support for the fact that victims of FMS are in fact are experiencing the pain which they report having.

Let us now have a look at a very recent case which examined all the issues arising in this area.

Maguire v Carillion Services Limited 31st March 2017 HHJ Main QC

County Court cases are of course not binding but this case is of some interest as the Court accepted the link between fibromyalgia and trauma. The Claimant, aged 58 years of age was employed by HMRC as a Higher Auditor. On 25th November 2011, a scenic lift suffered interference and damage. It juddered and jumped about as the Claimant ascended in it to the second floor. The Claimant's feet left the floor several times, although she did not fall and remained standing throughout. Liability was conceded. The Claimant presented with physical and psychological injuries. She became aware suddenly of an intense and fast vibration passing through her body which culminated in what felt like "an explosion". The lift having shuddered to a halt then continued upwards and the doors then opened at the second floor. The Claimant felt in severe shock and had to force herself to move her feet to step out. By then, all her muscles were shaking like jelly. She thought there had been a bomb and was terrified that the lift was going to fall. She then used the stairs to descend back to the ground floor and saw glass on the ground.

What had happened is that a window which could open inward into the scenic lift shaft had obstructed the passage of the lift and caused the window to break and the lift's path to be interrupted. The Claimant had not been struck by any debris. An ambulance was called and the claimant was said to be suffering from pins and needles in her arms and legs which dissipated. The Claimant then began to suffer from lumbar pain. The Claimant did not recover fully and kept a "pain diary".

5 Days after the accident, the claimant had to descend stairs at home on her bottom. Her ankles and knees were now giving way. She became incapable of day to day activities. Her neck and shoulders became painful as did her hips and she had to take extra pain relieving medication. The Claimant however attended a gym on 19th December 2011 and filled in a medical screening questionnaire and made no mention of any ill health or complaint. Her answers were inconsistent with her contemporary reporting in the diary. By 23rd December 2011 the Claimant was complaining of multi-level spinal pain and she underwent an MRI scan in January 2012 which showed minor degenerative changes at the C5/6 but no abnormalities or cord compression to account for her symptoms.

On 26th May 2012, she then suffered a road traffic accident when she was struck from behind by a third party causing £2613 of damage to her vehicle. She told experts her neck and back pain from the lift accident had not resolved prior to the car accident though it had "eased off". She said it had been aggravated by the 2012 road traffic accident. A treating rheumatologist diagnosed fibromyalgia in January 2013 and in March 2013 the lift accident was recorded as having triggered this.

There was an important pre-accident psychiatric history. The claimant had suffered physical and sexual abuse at the hands off her older sister between 3 and 7–8 years of age.

The Claimant in 1988 had felt odd sensations of dizziness and underwent a CT brain scan. An EEG suggested abnormality in the temporal lobes and the symptoms were put down to a presentation of temporal lobe epilepsy. There was also a pre-accident history of pain in different locations, back pain, left wrist pain and no history of trauma. There were other complaints where no organic cause for complaint was found. The Claimant also had several previous accidents which resulted in claims being intimated to insurance companies, in 2005, 2007, 2009 and 2012.

The Claimant's case was that the fibromyalgia had been triggered by the lift accident. The Defendant's case was that the Claimant had at most suffered a minor soft tissue injury and short term aggravation of pre-existing fibromyalgia and that her condition was fabricated, fraudulent and the product of deliberate or serious exaggeration for the motive of financial gain. The Defendant relied on extensive surveillance evidence. Far from being agoraphobic, the Claimant could go outside, go to the shops unaccompanied and displayed very little difficulty in her movements bending at the waist and rotating her neck freely. She engaged in lifting large bottles of coke without hesitation and could carry bags of shopping as well as wheeling a trolley. On one occasion, she was carrying a stick but placing no weight through it. When she was with friends from the FMS society her mobility was generally laboured in keeping with them but when separated from them the Claimant regained her normal ambulation ability and appeared to mobilise normally. The Defendant said this was a sure sign of deliberate exaggeration for financial gain.

The Claimant explained this by accepting what the surveillance showed but denied that it was inconsistent or showed exaggeration or malingering. The filming was misleading said the claimant and deliberately selective in filming or editing to give a misleading impression. The Judge was invited to be sceptical of the filming.

The Judge then heard from specialists in four fields, cardiac, orthopaedic, rheumatological and psychiatric. The differences of opinion were in respect of the rheumatologists and the psychiatric experts. The psychiatrists agreed that the Claimant's pre-accident history rendered her "vulnerable" to psychiatric disorder. They could not agree whether she was suffering from Somatic Symptom Disorder, (the new chapter in DSM V). Dr Bass for the Claimant thought she was and Professor Green instructed by the Claimant thought not. Professor Green thought that if there was a physical diagnosis he could not safely attach a SSD label. Dr Bass thought many of her complaints did not have an adequate physical organic explanation.

The rheumatologists, were Dr McKenna and Dr Huskisson. They agreed that the claimant suffered from FMS and that only limited improvement was expected. They agreed she was vulnerable to developing FMS. They couldn't agree however whether the Claimant was displaying FMS symptoms before the accident which would suggest that FMS was always likely to recur depending on life's stresses in the future. They could also not agree upon whether the surveillance presented suggested exaggeration.

The Judge then dealt with the allegations and pleading of fraud and found that the Defendant had not sufficiently pleaded the fraud allegations in sufficient detail to comply with the rules on pleading.

The Judge found the Claimant to be a "confident and well prepared" witness. She looked to be in discomfort in the witness box. The Judge heard evidence from her family members and found both sons to be "impressive" witnesses as were her friends.

The Judge found that the Claimant had not suffered any pathological damage to her soft tissues because of the accident and relied on MRI to exclude this. He thought the differential diagnosis was 1) Deliberate exaggeration, 2) an overlaying functional presentation and/or (3) FMS.

The Judge reviewed the literature in relation to FMS and compared a study by Wolfe, Hauser et al *"Fibromyalgia and Physical Trauma"* Journal of Rheumatology 12/8/14 and a study by McLean Williams and Clauw *"Fibromyalgia after motor vehicle collision,* 1995. The Judge observed that some thought the trauma a trigger for central sensitisation and others thought it to be a stressor which caused widespread pain or somatic symptoms because of biological vulnerability. The judge said that hard evidence to support a clear association remains lacking. The Judge also observed that childhood sexual abuse and physical abuse had been well documented and was likely to be relevant to the development of FM and CFS. The Borsini et al study supports this view.

He found that there was no single event that gives rise to FMS but that it is a condition that evolves over time because of enduring sleep deprivation and fatigue. The Judge found that the pre-existing complaints of pain at various locations was SSD rather than previous FMS.

The judge in relation to the surveillance found that FMS is not a static condition and its effects would fluctuate depending on several variables, any increasing stress or anxiety, the extent of given sleep disturbance and the levels of fatigue. The Judge found that the development of FMS is multi-faceted and an underlying constitutional sensitivity is plainly at the heart of it. The Judge found her to be highly at risk of developing FMS when there was a convergence of stress and anxiety leading to sleep disturbance and fatigue.

The Judge then found as follows:-

1. The accident was shocking and frightening but an insignificant physical trauma of no more than 3 months' duration.

2. There was significant psychological trauma- PTSD.

3. The Claimant did develop a depressive disorder of mild to moderate severity.

4. The Claimant was displaying SSD after the accident and the Claimant had a pre-morbid history of this.

5. The Judge found that SSD and PTSD could co-exist.

6. There was a significant overlap between SSD and FMS, the former compounding the risk of the latter.

7. The Claimant was significantly vulnerable to developing FMS but had not developed it before the accident. SSD and FMS were not the same conditions. The pain was not sufficiently widespread.

8. The Claimant's pain diary was subjective and not entirely reliable or complete. The entries were self-serving and selective designed to be used in the legal claim.

9. The Claimant developed FMS 4-6 weeks post accident against a report of physical symptoms, SSD and vulnerability. It ebbed and flowed.

10. At some point the claimant was subjectively exaggerating the effects of her symptoms. The filming did show exaggeration, a sympathetic level of disability when she was with her FMS friends.

11. The exaggeration did not mean that she did not have FMS however.

12. The Court rejected the Claimant's assertion that "The Surveillance Group" had sought to mislead the Court by selectively stopping the filming at times when she was about to demonstrate disability.

13. The Judge rejected earnings increases based on the chance of promotion.

14. The Judge held that the Claimant's conduct was very far from the type of case where she could be deprived of all her damages.

15. The Judge then valued the Claimant's case allowing £26,500 for Pain Suffering and Loss of Amenity. In total the award to the Claimant was £133,601 plus £69,941.42 by way of a subrogated claim to HMRC. The Claimant had sought damages of £560,000 but the Judge found that the FMS condition had been accelerated by 6 years by the accident.

The acceleration was used effectively to discount the claim. The Judge found that the Claimant was significantly vulnerable to developing FMS. He found that the Claimant was already displaying signs of SSD and that it was not the physical injury but the anxiety and stress combined with the effects upon her sleeping patterns which caused her to develop FMS. He also looked at the risk of her developing a functional disorder more widely whether FMS or a diagnosis of another name and found that the Claimant would have had to have stopped work by her 60th birthday when she would have developed significant issues with her health because of SSD or FMS.

Chronic Fatigue Syndrome

CFS has chronic widespread pain as a major symptom. It is not as prevalent as fibromyalgia with a prevalence in the population of between 0.006% and 3%. Other symptoms are as follows:-

- Non-refreshing sleep
- Memory/concentration problems
- Pain in two or more joints
- Muscle pain
- Muscle discomfort
- Difficulty thinking
- Sleep problems
- Fatigue after exercise (>24hr)
- Migratory joint pain
- Unexplained muscle weakness
- Intolerance to exercise

- Anxiety
- Malaise after exertion (>24hr)
- Sweatiness/cold hands and feet
- Light/noise sensitivity
- Headaches
- Intolerance to standing
- Difficulty in understanding things
- Sore throat
- Tender glands in the neck/armpits
- Depression
- Confusion or disorientation
- Mild fever or chills
- Migraine

A diagnosis of CFS requires the following features:

1. Persistent chronic fatigue (at least 6 months) or intermittent, unexplained chronic fatigue, which relapses, or with a definite start, and is not the result of recent exertions. The fatigue is not improved by rest and results in a significant reduction in the patient's previous level of activity.

2. Exclusion of other diseases that may cause chronic fatigue plus four of the following eight minor criteria that have been present concurrently for 6 months or longer, after the onset of fatigue:

    a) Recently impaired memory or concentration.

b) Pain on swallowing

c) Painful axillary or cervical lymph nodes

d) Muscle pains

e) Joint pain without swelling

f) Headache with a new pattern or increased severity

g) Sleep that does not improve after rest

h) Post-exertional discomfort lasting more than 24 hours[2]

So, what are the causes of CFS? Extensive testing has failed to determine any common psychiatric cause. Sleep studies also proved inconclusive as have endocrine studies. Again, studies using more recent advances in MRI techniques using 3 Tesla MRI such as those by Puri & Jakeman et al have reported significant reductions in grey matter volume which are consistent with the complaint of impaired memory[3]. There is no generally accepted medication which seems to work. Antidepressant therapy seems to be of minimal benefit. Again, the only evidence based therapy of benefit appears to be Cognitive Behavioural Therapy[4]. Sadly, the prognosis of this condition is currently poor with recovery rates varying between 0% and 37%.

In cases of widespread pain, it is a matter for the experts to determine whether the trauma of the accident has played an initiating role and what the chance is of the Claimant suffering the same condition at some specified point in the future either without trauma or because of some non-tortious trigger. It is to that difficult issue of causation in chronic pain cases that we now turn.

---

2   Source: CFS International Study Group Criteria 1994.

3   Puri BK, Jakeman PM, Agour M, etal. Regional grey and white matter volumetric changes in myalgic encephalomyelitis [chronic fatigue syndrome]: a voxel-based morphometry 3 T MRI study. Br J Radiol. 2012;85[1015]:e270-e273.)

4   Poppe C, Petrovic M, Vogelaers D, et al: Cognitive behavior therapy in patients with chronic fatigue syndrome: the role of illness acceptance and neuroticism. J Psychosom Res 2013; 74: pp. 367-372

CHAPTER SEVEN
CAUSATION

The Legal tests for causation

The first test a Claimant must overcome in establishing causation is the "but for" test. If the Claimant's injury would have occurred irrespective of the Defendant's negligence, the negligence is not causative of the Claimants loss.

Lord Denning in *Cork v Kirby MacLean* [1952] explained the test in the following way "if the damage would not have happened but for a particular fault, then that fault is the cause of the damage; if it would have happened just the same, fault or no fault, the fault is not the cause of the damage".

I am not convinced how much that explanation will help practitioners. It appears to be somewhat tautologous.

A problem arises however if when considering the question, the answer is 'I don't know', or 'I don't know for certain'.

Satisfying the 'but for' test may be difficult to establish where there are several factual causes to consider.

See for example the case of *Barnett v Chelsea and Kensington Hospital Management Committee [1969] IQB 428*

Facts:

The Claimant and two workmen began vomiting after drinking tea. They presented themselves to the Defendant hospital, where the A & E Doctor called failed to attend. The Claimant subsequently died of arsenic poisoning.

Law:

It was held that the hospital was not liable. The Claimant would have died of arsenic poisoning even if he had received treatment.

Robinson v Post Office [1974] 2 All ER 737

Facts:

The Claimant cut his shin and required an anti-tetanus vaccination. The attending doctor gave a test injection to check for allergy, but only waited 30 seconds instead of 30 minutes. The Claimant being allergic contracted encephalitis and died.

Law:

It was held that since a positive response to the test injection would only have been apparent after nine days, the Claimant failed on causation.

Kay v Ayrshire and Arran Health Board [1987] 2 All ER 417 HL

Facts:

The Claimant was given a massive overdose of penicillin whilst being treated for meningitis. He was admitted to ITU and made a complete recovery except for profound deafness.

Law:

There were two possible causes of action but one (the penicillin) had never caused deafness but the other (meningitis). The Claimant failed on causation.

Bolitho v City and Hackney Health Authority [1997] 4 All ER 771 HL

Facts:

The Claimant was a young child with a history of respiratory difficulties which appeared to undergo spontaneous recovery. During a third attack, when requested to do so, a doctor failed to attend. The child died. Expert opinion was divided over whether intubation by a clinician was required. The Defendant doctor stated at trial that, with regard to the child's medical history, she would not, if she had attended, intubated the child in any event. This was supported by expert opinion.

Law

It was held that the negligent failure to attend did not cause the boy's death and therefore there was a break in the chain of causation.

Key Point

The Defendant will only be liable if his conduct has caused the damage to the Claimant and that damage is not too remote in law.

Standard of Proof in Relation to Causation

The standard of proof is the normal civil standard – the 'balance of probabilities' i.e. Greater than a 50% chance that the Defendant's negligence caused the Claimant's damage. If it is more likely than not that an event was the cause, it is treated as if it were the cause.

In tort, where a Claimant has established that some recognised damage has been caused on the balance of probabilities, compensation can be awarded for other damage that might happen in the future by reducing the full amount payable in respect of the future injury by the probability of it occurring. One of the leading cases demonstrating this point is:

Hotson v East Berkshire Area Health Authority [1987] 1 All ER 210

Facts

The Claimant (aged 13) fell out of a tree and injured his hip. His injury was not initially diagnosed. Because of the Defendant hospital's delay in the Plaintiff's treatment, (as we then called Claimants) the Plaintiff developed avascular necrosis.

The trial judge gave him a 25% chance, that with proper medical treatment, he would have avoided the avascular necrosis.

Law:

First instance and Court of Appeal – He was awarded 25% of the damages he would have received if he could have shown that the avascular necrosis was caused by the Defendant's negligence.

The House of Lords – Reversed the judgment and held that the Claimant had failed to prove causation on the balance of probabilities. They said the once liability was established, on the balance of probabilities, then the loss to which the Claimant has sustained, is payable in full.

Successive Causes

This applies when you have a situation whereby a Claimant is injured by a Defendant's negligence, but, before the trial, an unrelated supervening event occurs which would have caused the same loss to the Claimant as the loss he is currently taking action against the Defendant for.

The law on successive causes was reviewed in the following case.

Murrell v Healy [2001] EWCA Civ 486, [2001] 4 All ER 345

Facts

The Claimant was involved in two separate car accidents some months apart. In relation to the first accident he claimed that it was feared that he might be unable to work again. But in relation to the second accident he claimed he would have returned to work within two months of the second accident. Further the Claimant claimed that the second accident had damaged his hips and knees.

The Law:

It was held that:

The Claimant should only be compensated for the additional damage the second accident caused to him as an already injured victim. This appears to follow previous decisions;

The first wrongdoer's liability is not reduced by the second tort.

The second wrongdoers were only liable for the extra damage caused to an already injured man.

The Claimant's hips and knees had not been injured in either of the accidents and from the time of the trial onwards he would be unable to work because of the damage to his hips and knees. This is an application of the Jobling approach that once one of the uncertainties of life, often referred to by judges as the "vicissitudes of life", manifests itself, it is to be considered. Thus, the Defendant was only liable for the damage suffered by the Claimant, because of the Defendant's negligence, up to the date that the damage to the Claimant's hips and knees would have made him unfit for work.

Where there is a successive accident therefore, you should ignore the happening of the second (or third etc.) accident. Consider first what would have happened in the absence of the second (or third) accident. If the Claimant would have gone on for example to develop a chronic pain disorder in any event of the same severity, then the second accident does not act as an intervening event.

Then consider the additional effect of the second or subsequent accident. The first tortfeasor is responsible for the effects of the first accident. The second is responsible for the additional effects of the second and so on.

To avoid inconsistent findings between medical experts, it may be better to ask for the same experts to report in both cases or if that is not possible to ask for the cases to be consolidated.

Exacerbation, Acceleration and Vulnerability

In a case of a claimant with a good health record and no pre-existing problems causation should not be difficult to determine. As we have seen in Chronic Pain claims, the Claimant will often have had pre-accident pain, psychological problems or unexplained complaints. Even more difficulties arise in cases where the claimant had some pre-existing related condition or vulnerability.

Experts need clear direction from the lawyers on these issues which is sometimes in my experience, not given.

The law in this area is complicated and often misunderstood by clinicians and sometimes by lawyers. It is often the case that incorrectly applied legal principles are a cause of confusion between clinicians and lawyers. There is also a tendency for the respective roles of the clinicians and the judge to become confused.

There are **three key words in use by lawyers, exacerbation, acceleration and vulnerability.** They are inter-related but have different legal consequences.

Exacerbation

If a claimant has a pre-existing condition or vulnerability, an accident may cause that to become symptomatic for a period and thereafter the symptoms will subside with no noticeable long term effects on the claimant. In such a situation, the claimant may claim damages only for the period of exacerbation.

Acceleration

It is often the case that a claimant has a pre-existing condition which is rendered symptomatic for a period but the underlying condition is also brought forward by a period of years. In such a case the damages are awarded for the initial period of exacerbation and for the period by which the underlying condition is brought forward.

Vulnerability

An underlying vulnerability for example the susceptibility to develop CRPS or chronic pain disorder can lead to a very different result. Let us assume that a claimant has an underlying condition which makes them liable to develop a set of symptoms but that vulnerability requires an additional factor before it is triggered. If we take as an example a psychiatric condition. It may be possible to say that a claimant is vulnerable to or pre-disposed to depression, based perhaps on their medical history.

In the leading case of Page v Smith (House of Lords) Mr Page was recovering from M.E. when he was involved in a traffic accident. It was a very minor accident but it caused him to develop a recrudescence of ME. Given his history, a recrudescence was always possible but required a *further provoking incident*, or perhaps may just have arisen spontaneously.

How should lawyers deal with such a situation? They start by ignoring the vulnerability and calculate damages on the basis that he would never work again. We then must assess the *chance* that the M.E would have happened again at some stage in the future either non-tortiously by a provoking incident and/or just spontaneously. If this future recrudescence requires a substantial event like a bad car accident or a fall downstairs, then we must assess the chance of that future event occurring. This involves assessing *when* it would have occurred and *how likely it is to have occurred*. In Page v Smith the judge reduced damages by 25%.

The assessment of how likely such an event is, is for the judge, but the description of the event that is likely to have such a consequence is for the clinicians. To complicate things slightly the event if there is one must be non-tortious but again that is for the judge.

How should experts express this?

If the situation presented is like that described immediately above, we do not express the view that the vulnerability is responsible for 75% or whatever of the damage as that usurps the judge's role. The Clinician's role is to help the Court with the sort of non-tortious event that have produced the symptoms in any event and the chance of the condition occurring spontaneously without trauma at a given time.

Here is a diagram showing how lawyers and experts should deal with the concept of vulnerability: -

Ignore vulnerability (take victim as find them)	
Assess 100%	Damages
⇩	
Discount % chance of happening anyway	
Ignore tortious events	Take into account non-tortious events
⇩	
Clinician – Tell the Court what sort of event	
Judge	Assesses chance of that event happening

Multiple accidents or impacts

In road traffic accidents involving rear collisions there are two common scenarios.

1. The first is where the Claimant has driven into the car in front and then suffered a rear end impact from the Defendant.

2. The second is where the Claimant feels two impacts from behind, one from the car behind and then a second impact from the car behind that vehicle which again pushes the car behind into the Claimant's vehicle.

The test to apply where there has been more than one impact in the same accident claim is the same test of causation. Lawyers and experts should not assume that each impact has caused 50% of the damage. Much will depend on:-

- The direction of impact,

- Awareness of the claimant and position adopted,

- Speed and force of the respective impacts,

- The Claimant's own perception.

Furthermore, it is worth remembering that a Defendant responsible for some of the damage is responsible for the whole unless some other Defendant has been brought into the proceedings.

Differential diagnosis

It is helpful to consider other possible causes of the injury complained of even if only to discount the other causes.

It is also acceptable for experts to tell the Court what their diagnosis depends upon, for example the evidence of the claimant being accepted that the accident was of the magnitude that he indicated or that he was subjected to a certain movement that he indicates he was or the veracity of the claimant. Pain of course cannot be seen (except perhaps now in functional MRI scans).

The causation of soft tissue pain from "whiplash" is complex and the diagnosis of chronic pain disorder and syndrome is even more so. It is acceptable and perhaps even good practice for experts to make a diagnosis which is dependent upon the Court finding certain facts or that the claimant is an accurate and reliable historian and is telling the truth if this is made clear in the report.

Duty of a claimant to mitigate losses

A Claimant cannot expect to recover damages for the continuation of his injuries which are due to his own neglect or where he has failed to take reasonable steps to reduce his losses.

The burden of proof on establishing a failure to mitigate is upon the Defendant.

In this context, failure to mitigate may be for example unreasonably failing to take treatment such as physiotherapy which would have got him better sooner.

The Claimant cannot recover for losses which he ought to have avoided

In relation to returning to work it is worth remembering that the Defendant must establish that not only is the claimant physically able to return to work but that such work is then available for the Claimant to do.

Minor road traffic accidents as a cause of Chronic Pain

It may be thought that only very serious road traffic accidents can generate Chronic Pain Disorder certainly at least pain of an organic variety. The suspicion generated in respect of chronic pain syndrome and a claimant's veracity is often sparked by the fact that often the initial road trauma is relatively minor, a low speed road traffic accident. It would therefore be amiss not to mention at all some of the factors at work in common rear end road traffic accidents.

It is always important to consider the mechanism of the accident. Indeed, letters of instruction to experts should always be as detailed as possible in this regard. We need to venture briefly into the world of physics.

Energy cannot just disappear; it must be dissipated in some form. In the most simplistic rear end collision, all the kinetic energy lost by the second car would be transferred to the kinetic energy of the first car as it is accelerated forwards. The energy dissipated *through* the vehicle therefore depends upon whether the rear of the vehicle is damaged at all. Damage to the rear of the vehicle means the vehicle itself has absorbed some of the impact. It follows that if the front and rear ends of cars are designed to crush and absorb energy, a smaller proportion of the energy lost by the car will be transferred to the kinetic energy of the first car. The first car will not accelerate forwards as fast and the forces experienced by the occupant of the car will be significantly reduced.

If cars were designed to crumple during the slightest condition that would be unacceptable to customers and certainly not acceptable to insurers. Consequently, designs of motor cars are such that there will be no crush in frontal and rear collisions where the impact speed with a concrete barrier is less than about 5 miles per hour. Concrete is much stiffer than a car however so in general there is no significant crush damage to cars up to closing speeds of about 10 miles per hour. This depends of course upon vehicle to vehicle. The front ends of cars tend however to be stiffer and more crush resistant than the rear ends of cars.

What is forgotten by many is that what matters is not damage to the car but the forces applied to the person. When the force is applied to an object it is accelerated. In a rear end impact, the torso is kept virtually stationary by the seat belt. The head is unfortunately not restrained and in most cases, ill-adjusted head restraints mean that the head restraint is too far away from the head or at the wrong height to prevent the head moving sharply. As the torso is accelerated forward, the head is left behind. Then the seat back initially loaded by the inertia of the occupant releases the stored energy and recoils. This results in a further impulse through the torso caused by the seat back which causes further injury. The neck rolls backward therefore extending the neck beyond its usual maximum extension ranges thereby causing damage to soft tissues. After flexing backwards, the head must catch up with the torso causing the head to accelerate forwards again. To do this, as the torso is accelerating with the car, the head must have to accelerate faster than the car up to 2½ times faster. The head catches up with the torso and the car starts to decelerate and the collision is over. The head then decelerates rapidly and the head goes rearwards again. All of this occurs in about 300 milliseconds. The average acceleration required to increase the speed of a car of about 1.3 tons to about 10 miles per hour from rest in only 300 milliseconds is 15 metres per second per second or about 34 miles per hour per second[1]. The injury is caused not by the average acceleration but by the peak acceleration which can be up to 5 times the average acceleration but is usually about twice the average. If the average head is about 4.5 kilograms engineers tell us that the peak acceleration of the head will involve forces of about 9g. Compare this with the maximum g-force usually experienced by astronauts during take-off and re-entry of just 3g.

Now, when you factor in that vehicles are becoming stiffer it may be easier to understand why there is a higher proportion of victims claiming that they have suffered soft tissue injuries.

The European New Car Crash Assessment Program (EuroNcap) tests have prompted manufacturers to introduce new designs and build to withstand the terrific forces released during the 40 miles per hour offset frontal collision. Thatcham, the research organisation has found that vehicles have indeed become stiffer. Furthermore, insurers now specify that cars should not be damaged visibly until at least 15 km/h. The level of damage in modest low speed collisions tends to be modest when compared to earlier models of car. Finally, ride and handling considerations have resulted in greater stiffness and rigidity.

When comparing a "crash pulse" from a 1983 model car with that of a year 2000 model car, the 1983 model peaked with a 6g acceleration force with a pulse duration of 100 milliseconds whereas the 2000 model peaked at 15g with a pulse duration of 75 milliseconds – shorter sharper shock and greater potential for injury.

When asked to describe the impact resulting from lowest speed rear end impacts it is a common theme that these claimants have described a severe jolt or shock.

In general, do not be surprised that an impact speed of 10 mph can produce some painful soft tissue injuries. Half of all whiplash type

---

[1] Meaning that if acceleration forces lasted for one second the head would be accelerated to 34 miles per hour

injuries occur at vehicle speeds of 6 to 12 mph. Generally, damage to the vehicle only begins to occur at the upper end of that range.

This is not to say that modest road traffic accidents all produce longstanding whiplash type claims let alone chronic pain disorder. They of course do not. Most injuries settle within weeks or months.

Evidence based research however shows that between 8 and 14% of such injuries do not settle within 2 years and that such pain may be permanent.

The facet joints are a mixture of bone and cartilage along the back of the spine. The facet joints are small stabilising joints between and behind the adjacent vertebrae and permit up to about 20% of the movement of the spine.

We cannot therefore exclude the possibility that sensitive nociceptors (pain receptors) nestled deep within the facet joints within cartilage can be damaged by these forces. Degenerative changes in the disc may be probably incidental. The miniscule damage or sensitisation to the nociceptors cannot be readily imaged.

Where nociceptors (nerves themselves responsible for pain) become damaged, then organically based Chronic Pain Disorder and neuropathic pain can result. It is simply not possible however to image the cause of such pain. Even the most sophisticated MRI scan, x-ray or CT scan cannot pick up damage to the capsule of the facet joint. Many studies have shown in fact that there is a poor correlation between pain and findings on an MRI (magnetic resonance scan image) so when some orthopaedic surgeons tell us that the pain must be arising from the degenerate disc, they also tell us that the accident itself could not have caused that but then go on to assume that the accident accelerated it by about 6 months to 5 years or so. The acceleration theory is a legal fiction. It is not taught in any medical school and I have asked numerous orthopaedic surgeons.

I am not sure therefore why they implicate the disc at all in the causation of the pain, presumably because they have not considered other explanations. There is ample literature to support these views.[2] Further, a review of studies by Charles Davis reported in the Journal of Forensic and Legal Medicine[3] found that the underlying chronic pain from whiplash injury could produce plasticity changes in different structures of neurones responsible for the amplification of nociception and exaggerated pain response. There was consistent evidence for hypersensitivity of the central nervous system to sensory stimulation in chronic pain after whiplash injury. Tissue damage often deep within the facet joint, detected or not by the available diagnostic methods was probably the main determinant of central hypersensitivity he concluded.

What is the other perspective?

There is of course an opposing side of the argument. Other literature has cited a poor correlation between speed of impact and the development of chronic pain. Other factors than mere physics must be at work.

Other biomedical studies have shown that there is a poor correlation between accidents which cause no damage. Soft tissue injuries should heal within a matter of weeks[4]. Some studies opine that the cause is

---

[2] Brault, Wheeler, Siegmund and Brault, "Clinical response of human subjects to rear end automobile collisions", 1998, 79, Archives of physical medicine & rehabilitation.

Castro et al, "Do whiplash injuries occur in low speed rear impacts?", 1997, 6 Eur Spine J.

Sturzenegger et al, "Presenting symptoms and signs of whiplash injury: The influence of accident mechanisms", Neurology, 1994, April.

Szabo, Welcher and Anderson, "Human occupant kinematic response in low speed rear end impacts", 1994, SAE technical paper 940532.

Szabo and Welcher, "Human subject kinematics and electromyographic activity during low speed rear impacts", 1996, SAE Technical Paper 962432.

West, Gough and Harper, "Low speed collision testing using human subjects", 1993, 5, 3, Accident Reconstruction Journal.

[3] Journal of Forensic and Legal Medicine 20 (2013) 74-85

purely psychological or compensation neurosis. We have already looked at the effect of litigation in this context.

We do know that some people however, do badly and go onto have long lasting and disproportionate pain. Those people often have pre-accident psychological vulnerability but the truth may be a mixture of organic pain and psychological vulnerability.

One possible explanation therefore is that in legal terms we are talking about a class of *vulnerable* people who have structures and functional alteration of the pain perception and amplification structures in the brain and spinal cord. In those people the stress and shock of the accident may re-awaken that vulnerability and may cause long standing pain.

I have also in practice noticed a correlation between the attitude of the Defendant driver or insurer to the Claimant and the outcome in relation to chronic pain. A strong feature of a sizeable proportion of claims I come across is that the Defendant was *abusive* or *aggressive to* the Claimant at the scene of the accident. This seems to have a particularly bad effect on the claimant where they were subjected as a child to abuse perhaps by a parent.

In truth, we as lawyers, and the Court are concerned with firstly, the veracity of the Claimant and secondly with legal causation.

Even if the precise scientific cause of the pain continues to elude the medical profession it is not a bar to recovery of damages.

The Courts can and should take account of vulnerability when assessing damages. One such case was <u>Malvicini v Ealing</u> which we will examine later.

---

4 *Biomechanics of minor automobile accidents: treatment implications for associated chronic spine symptoms.*Laborde JM, - J South Orthop Assoc - January 1, 2000; 9 (3); 187-92

CHAPTER EIGHT
BRINGING CHRONIC
PAIN CLAIMS

What does all this mean for the Personal Injury Practitioner acting for Claimants?

Firstly, it means that you must listen to the Claimant and not necessarily dismiss what they say in terms of the severity or long lasting nature of their injuries. It is often a good idea when you think you are dealing with a Chronic Pain Disorder claim to get specialist counsel on board early with the claim.

Before you do this, it is a very good idea to deal with disclosure as soon as possible. Counsel and the medical experts will need to see the ordered medical notes from the claimant going back to birth or childhood for reasons now which will be obvious to the reader. It is a good idea to ask the Claimant or a relative to keep a pain diary for the claimant. Asking the claimant to keep a diary is one option but focussing the claimant on the issue of the pain may be counter-productive to the claimant's perception of the pain.

You will probably obtain a draft medical report from a pain expert at counsel's recommendation and then have a conference to discuss the report and its findings

Secondly, you should be cautious about accepting standardised orthopaedic opinions suitable for the majority but not all of whiplash type or soft tissue injury cases.

Thirdly, you must be prepared to question the Orthopaedic Surgeon or General Practitioner about the possibility of a Chronic Pain Disorder where the signs are present. You should investigate further continuing pain going on beyond prognosis especially where there is no history of back and neck pain. You cannot assume that a degenerative disc is the likely cause of continuing pain.

Such evidence usually needs to be obtained from Chronic Pain experts, often Anaesthetists specialising in Chronic Pain and/or Rheumatologists or a Neuro-surgeon specialising in Chronic and Neuropathic Pain.

A draft report from a Consultant Psychiatrist with a special interest in Chronic Pain Disorder (not a psychologist who is not usually medically qualified as physician) should be obtained after or at the same time usually as the pain report. Where it is proportionate to do so there will need to be a meeting between counsel, the Claimant and the two or three experts at this point with all parties having a bundle of medical notes or at least a good summary of the medical records.

There will need to be cross-reading of the finalised reports between the psychiatrist and the Pain Expert and the Orthopaedic Surgeon. There are usually then recommendations for treatment. It is important to follow them as an accurate prognosis cannot usually be obtained before treatment has been tried leaving the claimant open to an inevitable defence that with treatment the prognosis would have been or is in fact very good.

Fourthly, therefore you should obtain timely interim payments for the Claimant for treatment where possible and referral to the Chronic Pain Management Team probably on a private basis. We have already seen that Cognitive Behavioural Therapy stands a real chance of successfully reversing the dysfunction in the brain's pain pathways. Talking to the dysfunctional painful brain can help.

There are now rehabilitation providers who specialise in chronic pain and some have considerable expertise in the area. What does not usually help is emphasising the disability and lack of function.

A graded exercise programme and hydrotherapy may be of benefit. In the most severe cases, an appointment of a case manager to help oversee the rehabilitation process and co-ordinate it could be useful but you are unlikely to achieve all of this without the co-operation of the insurer or an independent means of funding.

Many insurers now have specialist chronic pain teams with an excellent understanding of chronic pain. They deal with many chronic pain cases but you need to ensure that your case reaches one of the specialist experts usually in the complex claims team. This may mean highlighting your case as a potential chronic pain case in early course and asking for it to be transferred or looked at by a member of the chronic pain team from the insurer. They will usually appreciate the candour. What insurers dislike is being surprised at 3 years 4 months' post-accident with a claim now presented as a high value chronic pain case with a vast plethora of medical evidence.

The problem is that the more enlightened insurer knows that the best time to treat the claimant has passed. The value of the claim should not be the prime consideration. I would encourage more thought to the development of a specific pre-action protocol for chronic pain claims and a different costs regime which encourages more co-operation between insurer and claimant's solicitors. Good claimant solicitors should not suffer fixed or inadequate costs where the claim was complex and treatment has successfully worked to reduce the value of the claim from potentially catastrophic values. It is perhaps a mistake to align success and recovery of costs with the value of the claim and ultimate settlement.

The sooner that treatment is obtained for chronic pain disorders, the better the outcome. Pain which has persisted beyond 2 to 3 years is quite intransient and difficult to treat. Such pain is often permanent. Management of Pain on residential courses is an often recommended but expensive treatment. Too often this recommendation comes too late, 4-5 years into the claim and the insurer knows it is just another way of confirming the poor outcome and at some considerable expense at that. For this reason, they often refuse to fund such courses.

Fifthly you will need to prepare the witness statements as the case progresses from the claimant and family and friends. Photographs and video evidence of the claimant before the accident can assist in dispelling the "good old days" bias argument.

Malingering

Malingering as a differential diagnosis cannot be ignored in chronic pain claims. The capacity for malingering arises due to the compensation process and the lack of objective signs or evidence for the existence of chronic pain disorder. The process can be influenced by mood and non-organic factors. Claimant Solicitors should now ask at the first meeting to look at the Claimant's social media sites with their consent and in their presence, of course. It can be helpful to see how the claimant portrays them self and what activities they have been doing. Having done this, I once found a claimant who was riddled with pain and said they could barely go anywhere recently holidaying in Paris without any outward sign of pain or disability which was completely contrary to their case.

Part of the problem however is that Claimant's lawyers need to be sufficiently careful to elicit from their clients, the good days and the bad days. The tendency to portray the worst-case scenario must be avoided at all costs. The condition must be documented accurately and carefully and preferably contemporaneously and in the Claimant's, own words. The point is that often, Claimant's do try to express and impress upon people, just how distressed they are rather than actually answering the questions directly for example about how much pain they are in. Many claimants often reply that their pain on a scale of 0 to 10 is a 9 or a 10, the worst pain imaginable yet they sit in a meeting and don't appear to be in that sort of pain. It's unlikely that they are trying to deceive or they would feign greater outward expressions of pain. They are often confusing the question with how distressed the pain and overall alteration of their life makes them *feel*. A few choice questions can bring them back on track and help them to provide more realistic answers.

Witness statements

A word on witness statements. Witness statements are not statements of case and they are not an opportunity to regurgitate the contents of medical reports and import stock phrases from the Solicitor. Many witness statements I see are poor quality, insufficiently detailed and not in the witness's own words. Witness statements are hard work but are the lynchpin of a successful chronic pain case.

The timing of medication and changes of medication, injections, counselling and mood can all affect the level of disability and perceived level of pain. It is important therefore not to focus in a witness statement or schedule of loss simply upon what the Claimant cannot do but instead the Claimant must also focus on what they can do especially on the good days.

The format of the witness statement may be as follows: -

- Introduction and formalities.

- The brief circumstances of the accident and the claim to set the scene.

- The Claimant's pre-accident history employment history and health in chronological order.

- Some details of the accident and immediate pain and injuries.

- The initial days in hospital or initial medical treatment.

- Discharge from hospital and coming home or further medical treatment in the days after the accident.

- Details from the pain diary will help.

- Any worsening or progression of the pain.

- The sensation or type of pain.

- Any attempts to return to work and what happened.

- The attitude of the employer.

- Medication.

- Attempts to treat the pain descending into the detail.

- How the treatment helped or did not help.

- The detailed effect of the pain upon normal day to day activities.

- Effect upon the Claimant's ability to care for children, clean the house do normal daily chores, do the gardening, decorating, driving and so on.

The witness statement should progress in chronological order. It needs to be commenced when the claimant consults you and regularly updated, not 3 years 9 months down the line when the Court orders you to disclose a witness statement. That then becomes a mammoth task. It is not surprising that it is then not done well.

It is important to provide adequate information about the effect of the injuries upon the claimant.

"Pain and suffering" – it might be thought these were the one and the same thing except perhaps the same level of pain may subjectively cause different levels of suffering or "distress" in different people according to their subjective characteristics. In practice, there is probably little difference.

Loss of amenity – refers to the damages element to be awarded for the loss of the pleasures or "amenities" of life, whether permanently or temporarily.

The personal circumstances of the Claimant must therefore be reported.

Open ended questions can help prompt the Claimant to tell their story such as: -

"How did the injuries make you feel?"

"For how long did you feel like that?"

"What effect did the injury have upon you/your lifestyle?"

"What effect did it have if any upon your daily activities?"

"What effect, if any did it have upon your work?"

"How did you feel once you left hospital?"

"What was the journey home like?"

"How did you feel when you arrived at home?"

"What did you do when you arrived home?"

"Where did you sleep?"

"How did you toilet and bathe?"

"What did you manage to do?"

"Who looked after you?"

"What did they do for you?"

"When did you see a doctor or a nurse again?"

"What was physiotherapy like?"

"Which areas did they concentrate on?"

Look at the notes with the Claimant and exhibit appropriate documents.

Allowance can be made also for unpleasant surgical or other medical procedures that the Claimant had to undergo and these should also be reported upon. Don't forget to ask what medical treatment the Claimant has undergone since. Even niceties such as the size of the needle or pain experienced because of treatment can help the Judge form a view as to the genuineness of the Claimant.

Duration of symptoms

Ask the Claimant when the injuries got better or recovered. It is important not to suggest the answer but to use open ended questions.

e.g. "How long did you feel the pain?"

rather than "did it last 3 months?"

Ranges such as 3-4 months are more helpful than 3-6 months for example.

Don't forget to ask about the character of the pain e.g.

"What does the pain feel like?" Not – "is it stabbing or burning". That is leading the claimant and diminishes the claimant's evidence and may be iatrogenesis.

You could try and use important dates such as Easter and Christmas, or birthdays or summer holidays to try and establish the time frame. Experience shows us that people are generally poor at remembering or recalling time frames but do remember significant events and how they felt at those times. Ask to see social medial reports and photographs and even better, video footage.

If the pain is continuing, it is important to record at what level and intensity.

Cross reference what the claimant tells you with

- DWP notes

- Medical Consultations, both medico-legal and for treatment and with the GP

- Physiotherapy and CBT consultations

- Pain Questionnaires filled in by the claimant

Challenge inconsistencies, nicely but firmly.

Prognosis

If the pain is continuing it is important if you can do so to try and help provide a prognosis.

Is the pain improving at all? Does it vary according to season or temperature?

How stressful is the claimant finding the litigation?

What treatment has the claimant had?

What has the claimant been advised by treating experts?

Loss of amenity

It is helpful to ask the Claimant about how the injuries have affected him and whether there is anything that he has missed out on. Interference with hobbies or social life are of interest to the Court in valuing damages. Even an inability to take the dog for a walk, work in the allotment garden or visit his football club on a Saturday would count. Loss of or interruption to a holiday for example would be of interest.

Claimant's ability to care for herself

Care and assistance provided free of charge by relatives even in less serious cases can attract damages. There is no need for any agreement with the relative, the court can decide what sum should be added to the Claimant's damages which would be fair recompense to the relative.

Use the witness statement to help the Court understand what the claimant needed and why and who provided it. Obtain supporting statements.

Claimant's leisure activities and family life

It is helpful for the Court to have some background about the claimant, their living arrangements and family circumstances to assess the impact upon his or her leisure activities. For example, an injury may have a much more severe impact upon a busy mother with two young children who must struggle on regardless than perhaps a person with no dependent children.

Claimant's ability to work

Simple open questions such as "what do you do for a living"? and "what does your job involve you doing"? will help the Court and lawyers understand the claimant's work and whether any time off claimed is reasonably consistent with the injuries. You do need to go into the detail and understand what the claimant did.

For example, condescend to the detail of the job and whether the claimant for example finds sitting for extended periods very difficult or looking down at a computer screen or moving heavy items. Don't forget to talk about career progression and ask for evidence.

Surveillance

In short, surveillance should be expected and the insurer's expectations managed. In this way, it should be manifestly obvious at an early stage to weed out the few claimants who are truly malingering. Witness statements need to be taken frequently and carefully as the litigation progresses by the fee earner responsible for the case and with a good understanding of the case. A diary kept by the Claimant or close family member can also be useful in compiling that witness evidence.

Diaries can be useful to dispel theories of the "Good old days bias" particularly where it can be suggested that the claimant had an element of pain before the accident as well.

Care and aids and equipment are usually "light touch" In chronic pain cases to avoid stimulating the reward element pathways in the brain.

Similarly, it may be better to avoid presenting the claimant with very high value schedules of loss based on an assumption that the claimant will never get better in the claim before treatment has determined whether that is the case or not. Judges at Costs and Case Management

Conferences will need only to know the potential value of the case if the claimant doesn't get better and that can be advanced by way of skeleton argument or draft schedule, not signed by the Claimant.

Of course, if the case has been identified early and flagged with the insurer at an early stage the treatment stage should be taking place in the first year after the accident or even earlier.

In cases, which end up being issued, it is useful at the CCMC to ask for a date by when surveillance should be disclosed (the so called "Hayden" order) to avoid ambushes close to trial and to avoid additional expense. The Defendant is entitled to wait until the Claimant has "pinned his sail to the mast" however which will usually mean the time for service of a comprehensive schedule of loss and witness statement.

CHAPTER NINE
DEFENDING CHRONIC
PAIN CASES

The law is that pre-existing vulnerability is no defence to a claim. It may reduce damages however as we shall see. Just as some claims sometimes are poorly presented some are badly defended because of a lack of understanding of the law and the medicine. Many insurers cannot believe that such minor accidents can lead to such catastrophic pain responses and automatically therefore believe that malingering must be the only explanation. This is sometimes promulgated by experts and lawyers, who only provide their medico-legal services to the insurance sector. A balanced view and a deep understanding of the law and medicine is what is required for a good, just (and often cheaper) outcome in all cases.

In some cases, of course, malingering is the explanation, or exaggeration at least. When those cases are detected, the insurer client may well form the view that all cases are ones of malingering and it is only the minority which they catch. That is however against the research and the fact that chronic pain cases exist of course outside the litigation context.

Remember, stress of litigation and anger may be a strong perpetuating factor in pain cases and an empathic Defendant insurer can of course be part of the cure. Defending every claim as fraudulent or exaggerated can lead to a worse outcome for the insurer and for the Claimant.

It is only right however that the insurer should establish that this is a genuine claimant. Some evidence by Greve et al suggests malingering or exaggeration in between 20% and 50% of Chronic Pain Cases. If true, this means however that at least between 50% and 80% of cases are entirely genuine.

As we have seen we are probably dealing with issues of vulnerability and there are Defences and ways of reducing damages and showing exaggeration or fraud is only one of them.

Equally, I have seen cases where a hostile claims handler seemed to have initiated and provoked the injury in the aftermath of the accident. In that case both Claimant and Defendant were insured by the same insurer.

I pondered in that case whether insurer call centres need training on empathy and indeed whether the advice given to policy holders not to admit liability or fault has been misinterpreted as promoting hostility and has led to a failure to apologise and act decently in the aftermath of an accident regardless of who is at fault.

Remember that re-activation of the pain pathways because of stress and pain is one possible explanation for chronic pain disorders.

Fraud and exaggeration

Evidence of previous claims, variable history and presentation to different experts, only seeking medical help in the claim or since the inception of the claim and an anti-social personality are all probably markers which would justify detailed investigation of the Claimant's history and probably surveillance.

Alternative causation

Alternative causes of the pain and the timing and onset and presentation should all be carefully considered. The fact that an accident occurs in time shortly before the onset of widespread chronic pain is not determinative that this was the cause. A forensic examination of the accident circumstances, mechanism of the accident, and a detailed examination of physiotherapy notes, CBT and counselling notes, are likely to assist. I am frequently instructed on behalf of the Defendant with 10 lever arch files of documents in high value pain cases. After a forensic analysis, sometimes it comes down to one key page in the medical notes which show that in fact the Claimant was developing a pain condition even before the accident or that an alternative cause exists.

Pre-existing vulnerability

This is the key point in this area as we have seen. Even where the above defences don't apply, pre-existing vulnerability may reduce damages providing a partial defence. Comprehensive analysis of the medical notes and a good understanding of the medicine and the law is key.

Recovery

The Claimant's case is likely to be that the condition will continue for the rest of his or her life leading to substantial damages. Where a claimant has not instituted treatment properly or adequately then in one sense it may be easier to suggest that once the treatment has been tried then the claimant ought to make a degree of recovery. Claims which are hardest to defend are likely to be where the claimant has been through the full plethora of treatment both at an early and later stage and the symptoms have proved intransigent.

The Judge in Malvicini considered the Claimant's prospects of improvement as marginal and reduced general damages from £45,000 to £40,000.

It is always worth asking your experts however to consider the prospect of recovery and the effect of litigation.

If you are going to treat, act quickly. Consider whether further later treatment would be more effective after the litigation has ended. It is not unusual for the Defendant's experts to opine that the litigation is itself stressful and that treatment stands a very good chance only after the litigation has ended. Some Pain Management Programmes now refuse to take Claimants until after the court case has ended.

Best outcomes are achieved within 2 years and even earlier however.

Case Law – Malvicini

If you read just one case in the subject of chronic pain, let it be Malvicini. There is an absolute plethora of information in that case and almost all the topics and issues in this book are dealt with in the case. It was a hard-fought case on both sides.

In ***Malvicini v Ealing Primary Care Trust*** [2014] EWHC 378 QB, the Claimant a nurse sustained an injury to her upper left arm and scapular. Her case was that the pain was seriously disabling and mediated by mainly psychological factors. There was a large future loss of earnings and care claim. The Defendant's case was that this was the continuation of a somatoform disorder which arose because of exquisite vulnerability and that any minor accident or incident would have been a similar provoking factor. The Defendant therefore stated that the claimant in early course would have been in a similar position but for the accident. The Defendant also said there was a strong conscious element to the symptoms suggestive of malingering or exaggeration.

The Claimant had provided detailed witness statements dealing with her pre-accident employment and health status and background. She stated that she had loved her job and had been desperate to get into palliative care.

The experts all approached the claimant's condition from their own perspective. The orthopaedic experts couldn't explain it and called it "bizarre". The pain experts thought it was a chronic pain syndrome or chronic widespread pain. The Psychiatrists thought it was a conversion disorder or somatoform pain disorder. The Judge Robert Francis QC sitting as a High Court Judge however found the evidence of Dr Stone, a neurological expert of the most help. The Judge found that the disorder was both neurological and psychological probably not entirely discernible or known to medical science driven by psychological factors.

Three years on, we are closer as we have seen, to understanding with the benefit of functional MRI what actually is happening in the brain at an organic level. There remains much to be discovered however. The Judge ruled out malingering as a differential diagnosis. Such inconsistencies as there were, were explicable by reference to the Claimant's wish to communicate distress and the complexity of the condition. The Judge also formed the view that the claimant had not deliberately concealed her ability to take long trips to Brazil to see her family and in any event this was not inconsistent with her condition.

The Claimant in the end recovered around £766,000 in damages. The Judge deducted 10% for the vulnerability argument however allowing for the chance that the claimant would at some point have suffered a similar fate in any event.

Part of the problem was that vulnerability was not dealt with in any detail by the pain experts at all. In appropriate cases if the Defence is properly considered in accordance with the literature, I would suggest that there is scope for the discount for vulnerability to be much higher particularly where the inciting or triggering event is particularly trivial. It must be remembered however that it is not just the nature and the degree of event but the fact that somebody else, a tortfeasor, has caused the injury. The degree of distress and stress and anger are often that much higher where a third party has inflicted injury compared to the circumstances where nature is perhaps just taking its course or there is a trivial event for which nobody is to blame. The more serious the accident and the more stressful the circumstances of the injury are then it is more likely that the accident caused the condition complained of. Furthermore, it is less likely that the Claimant would have suffered the same condition without such stressful conditions being in place.

Practical Steps

Defendants should try where possible to Identify potential chronic pain cases early. Ask if the Claimant has got back to work for example. The following indicators are potentially indicators of a chronic pain case with potentially high value:-

- Continuing pain at 6 months.

- Claimant has not returned to work.

- The Claimant was just about to engage a lucrative/more lucrative career.

- The Claimant didn't enjoy work.

- There is a vulnerable psychiatric history.

- The Claimant is female and between 30 and 60.

- The Claimant has perhaps had more frequent consultations with a medical practitioner before the accident.

- Identity of the Solicitors' firm e.g. Fibromyalgia or Chronic Pain Specialists".

Rehabilitation

It is right to offer rehabilitation. It may ultimately save damages.

Therefore, it is worth offering an Interim Needs Assessment under the Rehabilitation Code

- The use of a Case Manager/Treating Physiotherapist specialist in Chronic Pain.

- Ask for monthly reports.

What do you offer

Psycho-social evaluation is important first. Psychological treatment maybe should come first or alongside physical treatment.

Treatment and Rehabilitation

It is worth remembering that both Claimant's and Defendant's representatives have a duty under the Rehabilitation Code to assist victims of personal injury with treatment. The goal of treatment should be to reduce pain while improving function and reducing psychosocial suffering. Treatments include: -

1. Ablative techniques

    There is evidence that Conventional or thermal radiofrequency ablation of the medial branch nerves to the fact joint should be performed for neck or low back pain when previous diagnostic injections of the facet joint have provided temporary relief.

2. Acupuncture

    There is some evidence that acupuncture or electro-acupuncture can provide relief for up to 6 months. The evidence base for the treatment of non-specific back pain is equivocal however.

3. Blocks

    Nerve root blocks in the form of injections have shown to provide relief in the short term. The evidence for use in the long term is equivocal.

4. Botulinum toxin injections

    This should rarely be used for myofascial pain. The evidence base for its effectiveness is poor.

5. Electrical Nerve stimulation

    This includes TENS relief. The overall evidence base for its effective use is strong and improved pain scores were achieved over a period of 3 to 6 months.

6. Steroid injections with or without local anaesthetic

    There is a good evidence base for temporary relief of pain where that pain radiates say to the leg. Scores for low back pain were not as good.

7. Minimally invasive spinal procedures

   Ideal where there is an identified lesion such as a disc which requires decompressing (where it is pressing on a nerve).

8. Pharmacological management

   This is the mainstay of treatment and evidence of past treatment is often found at a later stage in the Claimant's GP and hospital notes. Gabapentin and Pre-gabalin are often good clues to a potential diagnosis of a chronic pain disorder.

9. Physical and restorative therapies

   There is general agreement amongst clinicians that treatments such as physiotherapy, fitness classes, and exercise therapy should be used for claimants with low back pain and other conditions where possible

10. Psychological treatment

    Cognitive Behavioural Therapy, relaxation training, supportive psychotherapy and group therapy generally are recommended. Pain Management courses especially when all else has failed to alleviate the pain are often recommended such as those run by the Real Health Institute or the Walton Centre in Liverpool. The costs of these courses run into many thousands of pounds.

11. Trigger Point injections

    Generally recommended for muscular type pain but efficacy is usually limited to a matter of months.

Obtain the Evidence

- Obtain all the notes.

- This can be a tedious time consuming process.

- The overlooked notes are often the most important.

- The physiotherapy notes.

- The Counselling notes.

- The Pain Team notes.

- Why?

    - These are long Consultations.

    - They are frequent consultations.

    - They are non-medico-legal and Claimant's usually open up more.

    - There are often diagrams and detailed medical notes.

    - Diagrams and detailed descriptions.

    - Previous pain detailed.

In one recent case in Jersey, the potential £1m plus claim (with Discount rate arguments it had the potential to comfortably exceed this) was reduced to £350,000 by a careful analysis of causation. I had 10 lever arch files of papers. There was one note before the accident in the initially unobtained physiotherapy notes which demonstrated the same symptoms the claimant complained of after the accident, but 3 months BEFORE the accident. The Claimant's experts had missed it entirely as had their Solicitors and Counsel.

Don't overlook the potential to obtain witness statements from colleagues at work for example. Did the Claimant enjoy work? Have there been redundancies? Obtain the personnel file. Did the Claimant complain of pain at work or need special adaptations or conditions already? How much sick leave had the claimant taken from work? Examine contentions of career change to a more lucrative career a little sceptically. It seems to be a feature in many chronic pain cases that the claimant was just about to do better but for the accident.

The DWP notes also may help. They take a long time to obtain and the precise form must be used and it must be the current version. Always check that you have the latest version from the website of the DWP not the one stored on your firm's system.

Most firms of solicitors or in-house departments can obtain specialist intelligence material. I personally have found these more useful at JSM than surveillance evidence. The Claimant's self-reports of attending concerts with standing room only whilst riddled with chronic pain served to reduce the claim from over £600,000 to £150,000 at JSM in one recent case.

Malingering and surveillance evidence

Malingering as a differential diagnosis cannot be ignored in chronic pain syndrome. The capacity for malingering arises due to the compensation process and the lack of objective signs or evidence for the existence of chronic pain disorder. The process can be influenced by mood and non-organic factors.

Part of the problem (or maybe to the insurer's benefit) however is that Claimant's lawyers need to be sufficiently careful to elicit from their clients, the good days and the bad days. Frequently they do not or the Claimant is not sufficiently forthright.

The condition must be documented accurately and carefully and preferably contemporaneously.

The timing of medication and changes of medication, injections, counselling and mood can all affect the level of disability and perceived level of pain. It is important therefore to ask for early witness statements and/or schedule of loss from the claimant.

- Assume that every Claimant is now warned of the possibility of surveillance and is surveillance aware.

- Surveillance may engage Article 8 and is in any event expensive and often inconclusive.

- Every so often it just devastates a fraudulent or exaggerating Claimant's case thus proving its worth time and time again.

- Use your recommended companies who are reputable and abide by best Codes of practice.

- Expect requests for

  - Unused footage.

  - TASSCAR (unmanned) surveillance.

  - Logs.

  - Unedited Footage.

  - Witness statements from the operatives.

  - Hayden Orders – Latest dates for when surveillance must be served.

- Do draft a specific letter of instruction.

- Tell the experts what you know.

- What is it the claimant says they cannot do – provide sources.

- Refer to medical appointments.

- Tell them what do you want to know – Use a list!

- What is it that the claimant qualifies that they cannot do at times. Help the operatives with times and frequencies.

- Use Audio as well as video. What the Claimant talks about and how may be as important.

Conferences

Have a detailed conference with specialist Counsel.

- Allow sufficient time – half a day probably.

- Ask experts to attend in person or use video conferencing.

- Prepare paginated bundles of reports and notes.

- Give an indication well in advance of the likely number of lever arch files to allow sufficient reading time.

- Chronological order:-

    ○ Place the notes in order, oldest to newest notes – all mixed not separated by where they are from.

    ○ We want to know what is happening/being said in all spheres at a time.

The Defence

We must consider vulnerability, acceleration, and malingering or exaggeration as potential defences. We also consider causation and the prospect of treatment getting the claimant much better. Ask Counsel to draft the Defence in the light of the medical notes and draft evidence.

Don't file "stock" defences or if you do, ask Counsel to draft the Defence at a later stage before the CCMC in the form of an amended Defence.

The rationale for pleading fraud specifically is obvious. The Claimant (as Defendant to the allegations made) needs to know with specificity what is being alleged so that they can provide evidence in rebuttal. Primary facts must be asserted in the Defence. The Defendant must comply with the well-known authority of ***Three Rivers v Bank of England*** **[2003] 2 AC 1 per Lord Millett at 291, paragraph 83.**

> *"It is not open to the Court to infer dishonesty from facts which have not been pleaded, or facts which have been pleaded but are consistent with honesty…"*

In *Hussain v Amin & Chartis* Insurance [2012] EWCC 1456 at paragraph 18, Davies LJ stated

> *"If the second defendant considered that it had sufficient material to justify a plea that the claim was based on a collision which was a sham or a fraud, it behoved it properly and in ample time before trial so to plead in clear and unequivocal terms and with proper particulars".*

When choosing whether to find that a party or witness has acted fraudulently the Court will take special caution and care. It is not an enhanced standard of proof but merely recognition that in assessing what is more probable, the more serious the allegation, the less likely it is of having occurred. Therefore, to prove the allegation, more cogent evidence is needed. When assessing whether the evidence put forward by that person charged with the onus of discharging this standard, succeeds where what is suggested is factually to have taken place is inherently improbable, the Court may well to whatever extent felt to be appropriate require stronger evidence before being satisfied.

The Judge, His Honour Judge Main QC in the Maguire case found that:-

> *"I must allow for the fact that in the overwhelming number of personal injury actions, Claimants present to the Court with genuine albeit subjective accounts of their symptoms. Often to underline the extent of those symptoms, they can in effect over-emphasise the problems and down play underlying constitutional difficulties, to ensure they are properly compensated. This happens up and down the country and it is the skill of the court in separating out cause and effect in relation to the injuries alleged. However, this is not to be confused with the malingerer or the Claimant intent on deliberately misleading the Court- fraud. This in fact, although a matter before the Courts, is much more uncommon. Ordinarily, people do not seek to support and present fraudulent claims, although it is a well-recognised phenomenon. Where such facts are being asserted by the Defendant- the Court should look for some cogent evidence, to find such fraudulent conduct, as being the more probable explanation of events…".*

It seems therefore that the whilst the Judge found disparity in the surveillance evidence and even exaggeration he did not think it was so gross to elicit an intention to mislead the Court.

Many insurers are perhaps left wondering what standard of video surveillance would be sufficient to elicit an intention to mislead. I respectfully submit that video evidence should in such cases include audio as well. Highly directional microphones capturing what the Claimant says and leading to an unassailable conclusion that the Claimant is deliberately misleading people, or evidence for example that the Claimant is working when she has said at the relevant time that she is not for example may also suffice.

What is meant by fraud and "fundamental dishonesty"?

Fraud is used to mean "the invention and presentation of false or exaggerated facts usually for the purposes of material gain of oneself or another"

At one end of the spectrum it may be used to mean a Claimant who slightly exaggerates genuine injuries and losses. At the other end of the spectrum would be the falsification or gross exaggeration of injuries or even the staging of accidents.

It is important however to mention that there is a presumption of innocence in civil proceedings. Whilst therefore the burden of proving a claim is on the Claimant, the burden of proving fraud (which should be specifically pleaded) lies on the Defendant.

How the courts interpret "fundamental dishonesty"

"Fundamental Dishonesty" is a slightly different concept. Section 57 of the Criminal Justice and Courts Act 2015 provides that in any personal injury claim where the court finds that the claimant is entitled to damages, but on an application by the defendant for dismissal is satisfied on the balance of probabilities that the claimant has been "fundamentally dishonest" in relation to either the claim itself (the primary claim) or a related claim, it must dismiss the primary claim entirely unless it is satisfied that the claimant would suffer substantial injustice as a result.

A related claim is defined in subsection (8) as one which is made by another person in connection with the same incident or series of incidents in connection with which the primary claim is made. Subsection (3) makes clear that the requirement to dismiss the claim includes the dismissal of any element of the primary claim in respect of which the claimant has not been dishonest.

The attraction to a Defendant therefore of establishing fundamental dishonesty is that it will usually result in the dismissal of the claim in full and the Claimant loses his costs protection and may be ordered to pay the Defendant's costs (see CPR 44.16).

"Fundamental dishonesty" is not defined in the Act and is the subject of much debate and case law.

In Gosling v Screwfix, Cambridge County Court, 29th April 2014 (Lawtel) a circuit judge sitting in the County Court decided that although an accident had occurred and the Claimant had been injured, because he had significantly exaggerated the effect of the injury and extent of ongoing symptoms, this was fundamentally dishonest and he lost his costs protection.

A Claimant recently lost costs protection (called "QOCS") when the impact or vehicle contact had not actually occurred.

In short, "fundamental dishonesty" is going to be something more than minor inaccuracies or in claiming bus fares. It is likely to be something that goes to the "root of the matter". In other words, it may be difficult to define, but you know it when you see it.

General Damages for Pain, Suffering and Loss of Amenity

Case law is not that useful in this setting. There are few reported cases. What is clear is that damages are likely to be much higher than the amount usually awarded for simple mechanical back or neck pain.

The JC guidelines are the most useful source. It will be noted that the new JC guidelines no longer regard Chronic Pain as an add on Psychiatric condition (Category 3) but it now has its own category under Section 8. The factors justifying the award of damages are specified as follows:-

The factors to be considered in valuing claims for pain disorders (including CRPS) include the following:

- the degree of pain experienced;

- the overall impact of the symptoms (which may include fatigue, associated impairments of cognitive function, muscle weakness, headaches etc. and taking account of any fluctuation in symptoms) on mobility, ability to function in daily life and the need for care/assistance;

- the effect of the condition on the injured person's ability to work;

- the need to take medication to control symptoms of pain and the effect of such medication on the person's ability to function in normal daily life;

- the extent to which treatment has been undertaken and its effect (or its predicted effect in respect of future treatment);

- whether the condition is limited to one anatomical site or is widespread;

- the presence of any separately identifiable psychiatric disorder and its impact on the perception of pain;

- the age of the claimant;

- prognosis.

General Damages for pain disorders vary from £16,000 to £52,660 with uplift.

General Damages for PSLA for Complex Regional Pain Syndrome vary from £21,300 to £70,240.

Practical advice

It is important when acting for a Defendant to identify potential chronic pain cases at an early stage (as possible) and to obtain the appropriate evidence and deal appropriately with it. If there is evidence of the signs of chronic pain disorder or injuries are not settling within prognosis, the first action should be to obtain the evidence, instruct the experts even if only desktop reports and have a conference with Counsel. It would be usual to obtain evidence from a chronic pain expert usually an Anaesthetist but sometimes a Rheumatologist or Neuro-surgeon or Neurologist. A psychiatrist will usually be essential too and an orthopaedic surgeon should be the starting point.

CHAPTER TEN
CONCLUSIONS

My aim with this book was to offer the reader a more complete understanding of this difficult area of Personal Injury law.

These are my own conclusions from attending and speaking at Medico-legal conferences, acting for Claimants and for Defendants for over 17 years and sitting as a part-time Judge.

- Not all soft tissue injuries recover fully. There is a class of individuals who do poorly after soft tissue or bony injury and go on to suffer pain and disability, probably 8-14%.

- There is probably a relationship between trauma and Chronic Widespread Pain.

- It is not a certain one.

- The questions are still often whether the Claimant is genuine and what would have caused it anyway and when.

- Chronic Pain Conditions probably have a basis in the dysfunctional pain pathway processing centres in the brain and in hyperexcitability in the spinal cord.

- Experts of different disciplines normally explain or fail to explain the problem in the context of their own discipline.

- Currently, medical knowledge is hard pressed to explain chronic pain disorders but functional MRI is throwing light on the disorders and explaining them as dysfunction in brain activity.

- CRPS is a specific chronic pain condition where there is sympathetic nervous system activity causing various visible changes to a limb.

- Even CRPS conditions can occasionally be feigned.

- Exaggeration/Malingering occurs in around 20-50% of cases.

- This is usually quite difficult to prove and must be specifically pleaded.

- Obtain background checks and/or good surveillance early.

- If the Claimant is genuine, be nice. Be generous early on.

- A slightly generous early settlement can prevent the claim from snowballing into a much larger one.

- Rehabilitate – it's cheaper in the long run (sometimes).

- It should normally be "Light Touch" not sufficient to reinforce the disability.

- If the Claimant is not genuine – Fight. BUT Fight all the way and don't give in unless further evidence comes to light that you were wrong.

- Claimants are usually vulnerable.

- Vulnerability is not a complete defence.

- It may reduce damages however.

- So, will treatment.

- Look at causation carefully.

- Assess whether this is an aggravation or acceleration case.

- There is a prospect of recovery which can reduce damages.

- It is possible to defend genuine cases to sensible levels of damages.

Whether acting for a Claimant or a Defendant it takes a deep understanding of the law and the medicine.

MORE BOOKS BY
LAW BRIEF PUBLISHING

'Ellis and Kevan on Credit Hire, 5th Edition' by Aidan Ellis & Tim Kevan
'RTA Allegations of Fraud in a Post-Jackson Era: The Handbook, 2nd Edition' by Andrew Mckie
'A Practical Guide to Holiday Sickness Claims' by Andrew Mckie & Ian Skeate
'RTA Personal Injury Claims: A Practical Guide Post-Jackson' by Andrew Mckie
'On Experts: CPR35 for Lawyers and Experts' by David Boyle
'A Practical Guide to Claims Arising From Accidents Abroad and Travel Claims' by Andrew Mckie & Ian Skeate
'A Practical Guide to Claims Arising from Fatal Accidents' by James Patience
'A Practical Approach to Clinical Negligence Post-Jackson' by Geoffrey Simpson-Scott
'A Practical Guide to Personal Injury Trusts' by Alan Robinson
'Occupiers, Highways and Defective Premises Claims: A Practical Guide Post-Jackson' by Andrew Mckie
'Employers' Liability Claims: A Practical Guide Post-Jackson' by Andrew Mckie
'A Practical Guide to Subtle Brain Injury Claims' by Pankaj Madan
'The Law of Driverless Cars: An Introduction' by Alex Glassbrook

'A Practical Guide to Costs in Personal Injury Cases' by Matthew Hoe
'A Practical Guide to Alternative Dispute Resolution in Personal Injury Claims – Getting the Most Out of ADR Post-Jackson' by Peter Causton, Nichola Evans, James Arrowsmith
'A Practical Guide to Personal Injuries in Sport' by Adam Walker & Patricia Leonard
'A Practical Guide to Marketing for Lawyers' by Catherine Bailey & Jennet Ingram
'Baby Steps: A Guide to Maternity Leave and Maternity Pay' by Leah Waller
'The Queen's Counsel Lawyer's Omnibus: 20 Years of Cartoons from the Times 1993-2013' by Alex Steuart Williams

These books and more are available to order online direct from the publisher at www.lawbriefpublishing.com, where you can also read free sample chapters. For any queries, contact us on 0844 587 2383 or mail@lawbriefpublishing.com.

Our books are also usually in stock at www.amazon.co.uk with free next day delivery for Prime members, and at good legal bookshops such as Hammicks and Wildy & Sons.

We are regularly launching new books in our series of practical day-to-day practitioners' guides. Visit our website and join our free newsletter to be kept informed.